# HOLLY♀♂AKS

*Girl talk*

TRANSWORLD PUBLISHERS
61– 63 Uxbridge Road, London W5 5SA
A Random House Group Company
www.rbooks.co.uk

First published in Great Britain
in 2010 by Channel 4 Books
an imprint of Transworld Publishers

Edited by Mari Roberts
Design by Lynnette Eve / lynne@design-jam.co.uk

A CIP catalogue record for this book
is available from the British Library.

ISBN 9781905026722

Addresses for Random House Group Ltd companies outside the UK
can be found at: www.randomhouse.co.uk
The Random House Group Ltd Reg. No. 954009

The Random House Group Limited supports the Forest Stewardship
Council (FSC), the leading international forest-certification organization.
All our titles that are printed on Greenpeace-approved FSC-certified paper
carry the FSC logo.  Our paper procurement policy can be found at
www.rbooks.co.uk/environment

Printed and bound in Great Britain by
Butler Tanner and Dennis Ltd

# HOLLYOAKS

## Girl talk

## LUCIE CAVE

Books

## PICTURE CREDITS

© Robin Matthews: 9-10, 48, 74, 84, 87, 106-117, 140-141, 142, 164, 166, 169, 180, 183, 184, 186, 189, 224.
© Zoe McConnell/Danilo Promotions Ltd/Lime Pictures : 51, 77, 145, 227.
© Lime Pictures: 47, 54-55, 80-81, 120-121, 148-149, 192-193, 230-231, 247.
© Ed Waring: 76 © WireImage [Jen at Tric awards]
© Matrixphotos.com [Jorgie in grey dress]: both 118
© Getty Images [Claire Cooper]  © Splash News [Gemma and Jen]
© WireImage [Hollie Jay] © Capital Pictures [Jorgie] : all 119

With thanks to Claire Cooper, Gemma Merna, Hollie-Jay Bowes, Jennifer Metcalfe, Jorgie Porter: 52-53, 78-79, 146-147, 190-191, 228-229.


We would also like to thank the Malmaison Liverpool.

# contents

# introduction

Hollyoaks Village. A world where the girls are dip-dyed a perfect golden bronze, born with inbuilt hair extensions and have bodies that most of us would cut off our right boob for. That's what we think, anyway. In this book we delve deep into the psyche of the *Hollyoaks* girl and meet the people behind the perfect façade – discovering that, refreshingly, they've got as many insecurities, boy problems and niggles about life as the rest of us.

Meet Jennifer Metcalfe, aka Mercedes Fisher – charming, earthy, funny and 'couldn't give a monkey's' about who or what life throws at her. Here she opens up about losing her dad at the age of 15, the realization she had 'immense stretch marks' on her 'gigantic bum' and her unguarded thoughts about love, sex and never being afraid to be who she is.

Then there's Claire Cooper, aka Jacqui McQueen – wise, sweet, pensive and secretly a bit bonkers – she talks candidly about being dumped, getting called a 'geek' at school and jokes that she'll never be happy with her boobs.

Hollie-Jay Bowes, aka Michaela McQueen – upbeat, maverick and wildly honest. In these pages she confesses to being 'clueless' when it comes to boys, remembers her childhood as 'an ugly ginger freak' and poignantly admits how insecurity about her looks led to her breaking down in tears in front of her *Hollyoaks* co-stars.

Gemma Merna, aka Carmel Valentine – a glamorous, lads'
mag darling in public, yet referred to cosily as 'Nana Merna'
by her girlfriends on set. She talks about how dyslexia tainted
her school days, her near-career working in Selfridges, and
inadvertently meeting the love of her life.

Jorgie Porter, the last member to join the infamous *Hollyoaks*
family, as Theresa McQueen – infectiously bubbly, constantly
happy and endearingly open. She speaks about how her first
sexual experience was like a military operation, how she
needs to drastically improve her fake-tanning regime and
the realization that focus and determination are the route to
happiness.

My name is Lucie Cave and I am in awe of the super-charged
surrealism, the gloss, the glamour and the hyperbole of the
*Hollyoaks* world. Here I dutifully ask the questions that any girl
in their right, neurotic, nosey and fun-seeking mind would want
to know the answers to. I seek to find the real people hiding
behind the polished *Hollyoaks* veneer. And, to my relief, I find
out that they're just as normal and silly as the rest of us.

In this book we nose into their fashion habits, sex lives, body
worries and boy troubles to bring you the definitive guide to
the *Hollyoaks* girl and what makes her tick. If you're a girl who
likes a moan, read on. If you've ever wondered what it was like
to be an actress, read on. If you're a girl who's had enough of
being dumped and is still reeling from heartache, read on. If you
think your future is nothing more than the sum of you and your
cellulite, read on. And if you want some surprises and are willing
to relinquish those stereotypes about girls on TV who always
look impossibly perfect, read on . . .

# career climb

## chapter 1

From Hollywood to *Hollyoaks*, the lure of being an actress is strong. It's something most of us have dreamt of at some point. The difference being that some girls are born to be stars, others are born to write (or read) about them.

But believe it or not, the path to *Hollyoaks* village hasn't always been smooth for these girls. One of them worked in a make-up counter in Harvey Nichols for two years, another held down a 9-to-5 job as a gym instructor while a third worked as a lifeguard for naked people (yes, really). Five very different girls – Gemma Merna, Jennifer Metcalfe, Jorgie Porter, Hollie-Jay Bowes and Claire Cooper – with five very different routes to their dream job. They discuss how they nearly didn't make it, the nervousness of their auditions and having to strip off on camera for the first time. You'd think that turning up to school wearing no knickers might've prepared them for that sort of thing . . . .

# Hello Hollyoaks

## 66 When I turned up at my audition the producer took one look at me and laughed 99

*Gemma Merna*

---

### Were you a fan of the show before?

**JORGIE** I thought everyone was absolutely stunning and there was no way I'd ever get a part! It was when Gary Lucy was in it and Gemma Atkinson. I never ever imagined I'd get a part in *Hollyoaks*.

**CLAIRE** I didn't really watch *Hollyoaks* before because I was so busy at the time – but I turned it on one day and saw Jen Metcalfe talking in this really deep voice. It made my ears prick up because I wasn't expecting it – she just wasn't typical, nor was Hollie. They were sassy girls. I didn't know I'd end up playing their sister.

**GEMMA** I remember when it first started because it was so glamorous and different to anything else on screen.

**HOLLIE** What's funny is that we'll bump into people who used to be in the show and even though we didn't work with them we always feel like we know each other – like we were in a little club. I do that with Gemma Atkinson and she left before I even joined.

---

## How did you get the part in *Hollyoaks*?

**CLAIRE** I was doing a brief stint in *Coronation Street* and the producers called my agent and said there was a part coming up. I was lucky enough to have been auditioning for *Holby City* that week too, which helped the nerves because I went to the audition not really thinking much about it.

**HOLLIE** I had a part in *Grange Hill*, playing Dawn O'Malley, and one day I got stopped in the corridor by our casting director, Dorothy. She looked at me funny as if she was studying me. About an hour later I got a phone call off my agent saying, 'You've got an audition tomorrow for a part in *Hollyoaks*.'

**JEN** I'd got down to the last eight or nine for the part of Clare played by Gemma Bissix before this part came up. I'd only just got an agent again and was pretty lucky because it happened almost straight after. I heard they were casting for the McQueen family, so I turned up in some skinny jeans and a tight white vest.

**JORGIE** I'd got an agent just before I went off to be a hotel entertainer in Greece where I had to pester the guests all day! I remember my agent was dead mad at me because I'd got a commercial when I was away and couldn't come back. The thing was, at the time I thought I'd had no choice but to go away because there wasn't any regular work. In the end I came back 'cos I'd had enough – too many slimy men! – and within a couple of months I got called to the audition for *Hollyoaks*.

## What did you have to do in the audition?

**GEMMA** I'd been for the part of another character in the show and didn't get it so I thought I must be doing something wrong – so this time I made sure I'd done everything I could. I'd read the break-down of what they wanted and I was just so determined that the producers would notice me. So I went to town and dressed up in the sort of outfit I thought Carmel would wear – completely over-the-top and glittery, and I waltzed through the door with conviction. I had big fishnet tights, thigh-high suede boots, a little denim skirt and a gold sequinned vest top with a little shrug, hair up with this ribbon round it and loads of make-up. Admittedly I did feel a bit self-conscious but I thought, I want this, and I tottered into the room. The producer took one look at me and started laughing. And afterwards, once I'd got the part, he said that while I was brilliant at acting that sort of character, what he noticed was that I stood out. When there's a room full of people who are all going for the same thing – you have to get noticed. It was so amazing when I got the part. I never thought it would happen to me.

**HOLLIE** I remember just looking round at all the other girls in the audition and thinking: they are beautiful. What am I doing here? [Laughs] They all had legs up to their armpits, big boobs, tiny waists. I didn't think I had a cat in hell's chance. But with Michaela they obviously wanted someone who didn't look like a stereotypical *Hollyoaks* girl. I was told to wear a school uniform – all I could find was my old shirt, which had people's signatures all over it from when I'd left, and my blazer. Our school motto was AIM HIGH – we had it on a badge on our blazers. I had defaced mine and scrubbed out the A in biro so I was there in my old blazer that said 'IM HIGH'! I got down to the final four and then got told I had the part. It was great because I already worked there for *Grange Hill* so I knew the crew.

**JORGIE** I remember in my casting there were all these people wearing tiny skirts and tarty little outfits. But I had woolly socks and a flowery dress on – which meant I stood out because of it and my innocence showed a little bit. I had to read with the casting director. It was about a storyline where I had to flirt with Tony [Nick Pickard] – which meant I had to flirt with the casting director, who's a woman! Lucky we didn't have to kiss!

**JEN** Gemma was one of the first people I met and we got on straight away, which was great and really put me at ease because I didn't know anyone else there. There was no competition between us because we look so different. She looked crazy in her sequins!

**CLAIRE** I joined the show later on and remember I had to read a script with Jen. She looked at me and went, [puts on deep voice] 'Hiya, love. All I know is that you've got to be bigger than me.' And I replied in a really posh voice, 'Oh, OK.' I didn't really know what she meant; it was just all a bit daunting. We got the script and my bit was really long and serious, I had pages to say. Then Jen said, 'Oh dear, I wouldn't want to be you.' But luckily it worked out because we're both from West Yorkshire so I found I could do the same accent easily, even though I was a bit posher. I dropped my voice so I sounded more like Mercedes and basically mimicked her!

**JEN** I got the part on Friday and was filming by Monday. I was so chuffed – they called me when I was in the gym where I worked and I remember screaming down the phone and immediately calling my mum. Work let me go home early and I went out celebrating at the weekend. Not ideal when I had my first day on the Monday!

**HOLLIE** It's all last minute how they put the characters together.

**JORGIE** I was the very last to join and when I found out I'd got the part I was on set the next day. My character was just meant to come in to muck up Tony's life a little bit but they obviously changed their minds and kept me on longer!

## How did you feel when you first stepped into wardrobe and make-up?

**JEN** For the audition for *Hollyoaks* I'd done my hair really big and curly but the producers said it was too much like Roxanne McKee's [who played Louise Summers]. I asked them if they wanted me to come back in with it naturally straight as it looked totally different that way. But they said, 'No, don't worry, we'll just get you a few little layers,' and sent me to get it cut. I was excited about getting the part so off I trotted. But when I came home I cried my eyes out! My hair was so much shorter and to me it looked like a boy's cut. I couldn't even touch it – I hated it that much! I had to make my mum wash it for me. It's finally grown back.

**CLAIRE** When I was first in the show Jacqui had quite glamorous make-up – she didn't look chavvy or anything. Her look has developed more over time and it was actually me who said, 'I've seen a girl with her hair all scraped back and two bits pulled out down the sides' – so it's my own fault she looks so bad! [Laughs] I wouldn't change it, though. I think it works.

## How would you describe your character?

**CLAIRE** In a way, Jacqui is bigger in character than Mercedes and is really quite gruesome and hideous but she's fun to play. I like playing her because she's ultimately a good person. She makes the audience think and she isn't a typical *Hollyoaks* girl. I look about 5 foot 11 when I play Jacqui but in fact I'm 5 foot 5. People are surprised when they meet me. I've taught myself that you can be something different physically when you are acting.

**GEMMA** Carmel is very ditzy and blonde, she's lovely. But she does have a stronger side to her when she has to. I think when I was 17 I was naïve like her in that I didn't have much common sense – but that's life experience. I'm a lot stronger and feistier and wiser than her now; I won't take any messing about.

## Have you developed the character yourself?

**CLAIRE** Yes I have, and the producers have been supportive of the choices I've made. I based her on the people who used to live near me in Barnsley – they were rough round the edges but salt-of-the-earth types and would speak in a drawl. They were all a bit snarly. I had an ex-partner who used to snarl too so there's a bit of him in there!

**GEMMA** I have loads of freedom with Carmel too. Although the producers knew they wanted someone like Carmel, I was able to bring a lot of what I thought she would be like to the character as well. And I brought a bit of me to her also. I think that's what makes her character real.

**CLAIRE** Jacqui's brilliant. When I eat in a scene it's funny because I'm quite polite in real life, but with Jacqui there's spaghetti everywhere – I look pretty disgusting!

## Were you nervous on your first day?

**JORGIE** My first scene was with Claire and was this big long exchange of questions and answers. Then I was with Tony [Nick Pickard] and had to be in a towel and a little bra and knickers – that was so nerve-wracking! Especially with all the camera crew and men around.

**CLAIRE** I was really nervous. You can see in my first scene I had a sweaty top lip! With the exception of Jorgie's character Theresa, the rest of the McQueens had been there for a while and were already accustomed to each other. So when you come in as a new member you have to really work hard. I knew that as Jacqui I was meant to be the leader of the pack as well, so I was expected to dominate instantly.

**HOLLIE** I was more nervous about going into the *Hollyoaks* green room – we'd all seen it when we were in *Grange Hill* and it looked like this unknown special place for famous people. We were always too scared to walk down the corridor. It was such a big deal. Nick Pickard was a legend – and I was so nervous when I first did a scene with him. It was really weird.

## Did you gel with each other straight away?

**CLAIRE** When I first met Jen I thought she was so different to me, I didn't know how it was going to work – both she and Gemma, in fact. They were a lot more raucous and loud. I was much more subdued.

**JORGIE** When I first started on set I sort of sat back and didn't say much. I couldn't be chatty and confident straight away – partly because I thought it would come across a bit wrong. But the girls were so nice and dead inviting. I think they knew I was going to be a regular so probably thought – we're going to have to live with her anyway! Gemma is so kind and has good advice. I can talk to her about anything. She's a bit like a mother to me. Hollie-Jay is closer to my age than the others so we probably have the most in common and talk about things in more depth. We tell each other secrets.

## Describe your first screen kiss.

**CLAIRE** Nick Pickard was my first onscreen kiss. I wasn't scared but it was weird, looking back, because it was one of the first scenes I did and we had to burst through the door ripping each other's clothes off. I remember us waiting behind the door and not knowing what to say. It was all very professional – but now we know each other so well we'd be in hysterics.

**HOLLIE** Mine was with a guy who played a character called Wayne. It was a bit eugh, if I'm honest. His girlfriend hated me after that because I shouted at him, 'You've given me a cold!' when we were at a party.

**JORGIE** Mine was with Tony, Nick Pickard, in our 'sexy scene'. We had to kiss loads of times – Nick was dead professional about it, though. He was saying, 'Let's do this and this,' and I thought, wow, so that made me feel more at ease.

**GEMMA** Mine was with Kevin Sacre and I was really nervous. I don't think it ever gets easier either. All the kisses I've had to do onscreen are weird. It's always going to be odd because it's not a kiss to be nice, it's acting.

## Is there a rule about not using tongues?

**GEMMA** I think there used to be – but with frisky young people on this show I don't think there's any rules!

**JEN** If it slips in, it slips in! [Laughs] But if you have a boyfriend, or vice versa, strap it down.

**JORGIE** I was so nervous at first. I was like, 'Do we use tongues? Do we grab hair?' But now I've snogged so many people onscreen it's usually the other person who gets nervous. Sometimes I watch it back and cringe, though, because I know my mum will be seeing it!

## What about the first time you had to strip off?

**CLAIRE** [Laughs] I just don't like people standing behind me! I don't mind people looking from the front – it's more that the people standing behind can see bits I can't. I get all paranoid and think: what are they looking at?!, when in reality they're probably just doing their job and looking at the shot. [Laughs] My first stripped-off scene was with Nick [Pickard] but they give you these little nude panties to protect your modesty, which makes it much more bearable.

**JORGIE** It's tough when you have to get naked. I remember having to do a bikini shot when all these extras were around and I had to walk past them wearing heels – I'm not the type of person who enjoys doing that! Because they're all strangers they could look at you and think: 'She loves herself' – it's so cringey.

**GEMMA** My first one was with Leo who played Alec on the show. It's not nice but you have to just get on with it and get it done. I do fret a bit, thinking: I just want to get through this. But it is weird trying to be sexual with someone you don't really know.

**CLAIRE** There are clips on YouTube called something like 'Hollyoaks Babes' where they freeze the shots of when you're stripping off in the show! It's weird. They make me laugh, though.

**JEN** Mercedes is always at it so I'm used to it now. It's like a walk in the park! [Laughs] The most full-on scene I've had to do was in one of the *Hollyoaks Later* episodes. Mercedes was meant to have sex in a toilet with this guy. I'd never met him before and suddenly we find ourselves wrapped around each other in a toilet with cameras all around us! A proper sex scene means you're giving a lot away! So I went for a lot of biting his neck and hiding my face. The guy I was doing it with wasn't creepy or anything, he was lovely – so I said to him, 'Look, this isn't good for any of us so let's just try and get it perfect in one take. Grab me wherever apart from there and there – and let's just go for it.' The great thing about working on *Hollyoaks* is they make you feel so at ease, so it was fine in the end. And it looked amazing when we watched it back because it was so realistic.

### Was it embarrassing having to make all the sex noises?

**JEN** A little bit. [Laughs] But it was Mercedes having sex. It wasn't Jenny there.

### How do you learn your lines?

**CLAIRE** On my own at home – to the wall or to my cat sometimes! I have to really learn them through and through – unless it's a scene when I just have to say, 'Hiya' and then I know I don't have to do the homework the night before. But I'm a real perfectionist, just like I was at school. It does annoy me sometimes because I might have to be up two hours later than someone else but that's me. Everyone has their own way. I need to make sure the lines are ingrained. And also because I have to speak differently to how I naturally would.

**JORGIE** In bed the night before, which is why I never go out on a school night. I talk out loud. You just have to sit there and talk to the wall until it's gone in. I'm not bad at remembering my lines though – I thought I would be and used to stick the scripts down the arms of the sofa after we'd done a read-through. There's probably a huge pile of them still there on the set of the McQueen house!

**HOLLIE** Sometimes I'll look at the same sentence in a script over and over again and it just won't sink in. And the more you read a word, the stranger it looks. Everyone has blips.

**GEMMA** When I first started, because of my dyslexia I had to read my scripts a week in advance. I always have to work a bit harder, but I knew I could do it. The good thing is that I can memorize things quite easily, which helps with acting. It's funny – because even at school, although I wasn't very good at reading, I could see numbers on a board and memorize them in an instant. When I learn my scripts I can picture it in my head. Now when I have to practise I just do it by myself at home – Ian [her fiancé] has tried to do it with me but he drives me insane because he keeps putting on stupid accents for each character and says, 'Am I doing it OK? I'm good, aren't I?!'

**Have you ever been really hung-over at work?**

**JEN** No comment!

**CLAIRE** I have in the past, but I don't do it now – I think twice! I can't handle it any more. Sometimes there will be a night when we're all at a work party or an awards do and one of us gets the short straw and has to come in for a scene the next day.

**GEMMA** There was one night when me and Jen went out and I wanted to go home but she refused because she was having such a good time! I walked down the stairs about five times trying to get her out of there and she'd say, 'Yeah, I'm coming now,' but she didn't follow me! The next day I said, 'Jen, I'm really annoyed with you!' and she looked at me with rollers in her hair and a really pitiful look on her face and kept saying, 'Please don't be angry with me today, I can't handle it.' That was the only one time and it was awful but I felt guilty because I like to be professional.

**HOLLIE** There was one time I remember Jen coming in and I said, 'Jenny, you stink of booze!'

**JEN** [Protesting] There was a reason why! I had a family birthday and was called in all of a sudden! I didn't know I was going to have to be on set. I wouldn't go out and get drunk knowing I had to be in.

**JORGIE** I remember that day; you kept telling me I looked like a verruca! [Laughs]

**JEN** I just can't do it any more. It takes me too long to recover.

## Do you ever get the giggles and corpse?

**CLAIRE** Me and Jen get the giggles all the time. There was one scene where we had to unwrap this cat thing that was meant to be a money box – it was wrapped in newspaper and we hadn't seen what it looked like before we did the take. We had to do the scene, talking all seriously about this money and how we were going to get caught by the police – and as we started to unravel it we just saw this giant body and a pin-shaped head that looked nothing like a cat at all!

**JEN** We were crying with laughter. Even the crew were.

**GEMMA** I had the giggles the other day because I had these heels on with bright pink trousers and a flare on them and they weren't really long enough. So everyone was laughing at me because I looked stupid. And I can't walk in heels; I'm always falling all over the place.

**JORGIE** Me and the other school kids in the show are so bad for laughing during scenes. But I think I've learnt to control it now. Once it took me 14 takes to get a scene right – that was a really bad day. I probably shouldn't be admitting that, though, should I?

## What happens when you can't stop laughing?

**CLAIRE** One of our directors just says, 'Come on now, girls!' and you think: right, I've got to think bad thoughts here. You're meant to say to yourself: 'I am being serious!' and apparently that helps. [Laughs]

**GEMMA** It depends who you're with – the worst person is Kent Riley [plays Zak Ramsey]. He's the funniest person you could ever meet, so once you work with him it's really hard to control it.

**JEN** But if you don't stop you end up having to stay till about nine at night to get the scene done!

**GEMMA** There was once when me and Nicole were doing a scene and Myra was making Carmel do something naughty to stitch Dom up. I had to react so much that I said, 'I feel like Dr Evil off *Austin Powers,*' and Nicole started doing the laugh and she was very good at it . . . then we did her single shot and right at the end of the take she suddenly did the laugh so seriously I couldn't believe she had done it. I was creased up laughing. The whole crew couldn't breathe for laughing! Then the director came over and said, 'I never said you could do that, Nicole.' It was the funniest thing ever.

## Do things ever go wrong on set?

**GEMMA** Yes! Once I was doing a scene where Carmel is meant to come barging through the door but the family were hiding stuff from her so the door was on the chain. But in the scene I ran at the door and was obviously stronger than I thought, because the chains came off and I fell straight in! It took ages for the crew to put them back on the door again. Everyone was in hysterics because it was like I was some heifer! And the other day I had a party scene where I had to storm out but there was this wedge outside the door and because I was wearing heels I tripped and fell flat on my face! I grazed my knee and I was crying. I'm always falling over – I'm terrible.

# Work and play

## **"** Claire sleepwalks and came in my room in the middle of the night! **"**

*Jorgie Porter*

---

**Do any of you live together?**

---

**HOLLIE** I moved out of home when I was 17 and I lived with Nathalie Emmanuel [who plays Sasha] for a while but I'm back with my mum now. And I absolutely love it. The bed sheets are always clean and the dogs are always walked. It's amazing.

**CLAIRE** I used to live with James Sutton who played our brother [now in *Emmerdale*], and then until a few months ago I lived with Jorgie.

**JORGIE** Living with Claire was so much fun. We did this dance-off in the house once – my boyfriend was watching telly and we started dancing in front of him as if we were trying to get his attention. We got really giggly. I'm so close to Claire now that I know what she's thinking. It's strange.

**JEN** I used to live with Gemma, and now Melissa who plays Loretta lives with me.

**CLAIRE** I loved living with Jorgie – we just giggled all the time. She was living with a really weird landlady at first and I suggested she moved in with me. Her boyfriend lived with us too but it wasn't like I was living with a couple, it was great fun.

**JORGIE** I lived there for about four months, didn't I? And it's true, my boyfriend Tom did pretty much move in – but it was really nice. We'd get dead excited about TV programmes that were on like *Big Brother*, and Claire would make us tea sometimes. Her cooking was dead, dead nice – her roasts especially. Sometimes we'd go for nights out in Manchester too. Occasionally she'd come home and I'd be bright orange from my fake tan and she'd be like, 'Whoa!' Tom and I live on our own now – which is nice because there's much more space.

**JEN** If I'm honest I like living on my own. I feel like a mum because I always want the flat to be tidy when I get back home – otherwise I can't relax. I think I've got OCD.

**CLAIRE** At least you're honest about it to people – you always warn potential flatmates. I still say good luck to the person who's going to live with you. [Laughs]

**JEN** When I lived with my ex years ago in Bradford, it didn't bother me so much. I think it's since I got older.

**CLAIRE** I'm a bit more laid-back than you.

**JEN** I'd like to give your kitchen a good tidy, though.

**CLAIRE** My kitchen's fine! You said it was neat the other day.

**JEN** It's a lot tidier than it was when Jorgie was living there.

**CLAIRE** That's the problem with having a small kitchen. I haven't got enough room in my cupboards to put everything away so I have to have a tray with bottles of vinegars and stuff.

**You should get Jen round to do your cleaning for you.**

**JEN** I actually don't get wound up at other people's mess as much as mine – when Jorgie was there it made me feel cosy that there was stuff about.

**CLAIRE** I put everything into little piles instead of putting it away – like bills I have to pay – or if Jorgie had left a pair of socks out I'd probably have put them in a pile too.

**Do you have house rules?**

**GEMMA** I would always tell any girls I know to go out with a guy who has OCD – don't live with a boy who's messy, even though I do! When someone's messy, it drives you insane. I don't let anyone wear shoes in my house – everyone has to wear slippers!

**CLAIRE** My only rules were don't smoke in the house and clean the bathroom. But no one ever looks after your space as well as they look after their own.

**JEN** I'm awful when I come round to yours!

**CLAIRE** The other day she came over and ordered a load of pizzas and I said, 'Babe, can you make sure you take those boxes out when you leave?' and she didn't! And I was lying on my couch the other day and I thought: what's that smell?

**JEN** [Laughs] It's quite disrespectful, isn't it? I have mine like a palace.

**GEMMA** I like getting all the nice bedding out for my mates when they come to stay. The problem is that my place is a bit out in the sticks, which makes it harder for people to come over. So I try and tempt people with cakes – the girls call me Nana Merna because I buy nice things for them. I said to Jen the other day, 'Do you want to come round for the weekend and I'll look after you.'

## Do you have any pets?

**GEMMA** I've got three dogs – Cole and Paige are both St Bernard's and then I've got Phoebe who's my Westie who's two years old. They're amazing, they just cuddle me all the time.

**CLAIRE** I have a clinically obese cat called Puscha. She was a rescue cat and she's just like a human – I can communicate with her.

**JEN** She's weird. She doesn't like me. I've got two Persian cats – Bella and Terry.

**CLAIRE** Bella's got an overbite.

**JEN** I paid a fortune for her.

**CLAIRE** And she's probably inbred!

**HOLLIE** I've got a dog called Isaac who's a pug and a Jack Russell mixed – he's got a huge underbite, he can't close his mouth properly. And he has a Mohican and it gets dyed different colours on his birthday and at Christmas. I can get him to sit, roll over, go left and go right. I trained him with my ex-boyfriend. At one point I taught him to jump when I said, 'Star Wars'!

## Have you got any bad habits?

**CLAIRE** I sleepwalk really badly. Sometimes I can control it but it's bad. Jorgie's experienced it.

**JORGIE** Yeah! One time she came into my room in the night and I knew she was sleepwalking so I hid under my duvet pretending I was fast asleep – I was a bit scared actually! I think she turned the telly on and off. Then another time I walked out to go to the toilet in the night and I was naked – and she walked out in her pyjamas. We'd met in the corridor and I was like, 'I'm naked!' and she went, 'I'm just, er, trying to find out what time I'm working tomorrow.'

### And she was asleep?

**JORGIE** Yes! And I said, 'Why do you want to find that out now?' So I just ran past her dead quick and she shot upstairs!

**CLAIRE** I sometimes wonder if I'm just seeing ghosts. I always convince the people I'm with that I'm awake. I often do scenes from scripts in my sleep! Boyfriends have been hit – I've jumped up and down on them, I've screamed. My friend stayed with me recently and I told her there was a man upstairs and took a duvet up to him! She was lying on the bed thinking: what man?

### Do you hang out much off set?

**GEMMA** When the *Hollyoaks* girls go out we paint the town red. I'm a bit of a party animal, but Jennifer Metcalfe is the biggest party girl out of all of us! We all have a great time when we go out. We love a bottle of wine and we do like our strawberry Bellinis.

**JEN** Me and Gemma clicked straight away and have hung out ever since. Claire was a bit more reserved; she'd not been out for about two years! So we had to get her out on the town.

**CLAIRE** I have to interrupt there and say the reason I was like that was due to a boy who'd messed my head up. But there wasn't a lot of effort needed for me to fit in with Gem and Jen. We became good friends and started hanging out really quickly.

**HOLLIE**: Because I live in Manchester it's harder for me to go out with the others after work but I see Jorgie quite a bit. I am rubbish at dancing and Jorgie obviously loves it because of her dance background. So she sent me to a street-dancing lesson to get rhythm. I went to a club with her afterwards and got on the dance floor and she started clapping – she was so proud!

**CLAIRE** Jen, Gemma and I see each other loads out of work. And even when we're back home at Christmas we try and meet up if we can – because Jen's in Leeds and I'm in Wakefield it means we're not far from each other. But most of the time we get really lazy and can't be bothered to move! There will be a few texts: 'What you doing?' 'Not much.' 'Do you want to do anything?' 'No.' We're such slobs!

**JORGIE** I don't hang out loads off set but when I do it's so much fun. I love it when we're all at a club because it's just crazy – like me and Jen dancing stupidly together on the dance floor. I love Jen's outgoing nature. She never takes things too seriously.

**HOLLIE** I'm in a band as well. At the moment it's a bit difficult because I'm working long hours and the other band members are at uni, so they'll email me a track and I'll work on the melody and send it back. But when work's not so hectic we rehearse about twice a week. I absolutely love it. We're called Jeanie in the Radiator.

**EN** When are we going to get to see you?

**HOLLIE** We're still working on material before we start gigging – but soon hopefully. You'll have to make sure you don't heckle though!

## Do you go on holiday together?

**EN** Loads. We went to Dubai last year.

**CLAIRE** We go away on so many holidays!

**EN** Remember Monte Carlo!?

**CLAIRE** Oh, that was hilarious.

**EN** It was kind of a last-minute thing – everywhere else was booked up and we'd always wanted to go to Monte Carlo. It wasn't the time of year when it was properly hot so we just chilled out all the time. And one of the days we decided we wanted to go for a spa . . .

**CLAIRE** Bearing in mind it is very posh out there so it was going to be one of the most luxurious spas we were ever likely to go to.

**JEN** So we went and booked this three-treatment package and we were stood on this balcony on the top of the terrace in our gowns going, 'This is alright, this, isn't it?'

**CLAIRE** Except we were surrounded by women who were dripping in diamonds.

**JEN** All proper posh! Then we went for a mud wrap, which I thought was going to be really relaxing but it was so claustrophobic!

**CLAIRE** I was pissing myself laughing because I knew what she'd be doing in the next room.

**JEN** And I was laughing because they were slapping mud all over me and I knew Claire wouldn't get her bits out 'cause she's a prude.

**CLAIRE** Then we had this weird underwater massage and they were spraying you all over the place and we were in hysterics.

**JEN** After that we had these robes on and were waltzing around. Then we were about to go and have a full body massage and I took off my gown and suddenly saw this patch of red. [Pauses] I was on my period and it had gone through!

**CLAIRE** When I came out of my massage I was like, 'That was lovely, wasn't it?' because I didn't know, and she was grimacing, 'I've got my period – we need to go.'

**JEN** I'd been walking round the spa with it trickling down my leg! There was even a bit on my slippers where it had dripped. Afterwards I got in the lift and there were drips of blood in there too. It was mortifying. Can you believe that happened in the poshest place ever?

**CLAIRE** It was a bit of a weird day, all in all. After that I wanted to go exploring the place so we went up all these steps . . .

**JEN** I hate walking – she'd dragged me!

**CLAIRE** And we met this guy who came over and out of the blue told us he did movies and that we were 'really interesting'.

**JEN** Turns out they were porno movies!

**CLAIRE** It was hilarious.

**JEN** He didn't recognize us from *Hollyoaks* or anything – he obviously just thought, 'They look like a pair of dirt bags.' [Laughs]

**CLAIRE** We had massage oil in our hair, which didn't help!

**JEN** We've also been to Dubai a few times.

**CLAIRE** We stayed in this resort that was full of honeymooning couples. I sat and had breakfast every morning on my own like a loner because Jen hates having breakfast.

**JEN** Remember that nightclub we went to?

**CLAIRE** Oh yeah! We were really going for it on the dance floor – there was R'n'B playing – and what we didn't realize is that prostitutes dance there to show off their wares! Some guy had gone over to one of our mates and said, 'How much for the two of them?'

**JEN** [Laughs] We were there breaking it down!

# School rules

## " I hated school. I never fitted in at all. I was the odd one "

*Gemma Merna*

## What were you like at school?

**JEN** I was quite good at school and kind of sat in the middle of the groups. I'd stick up for people who got bullied but I was accepted by the cool kids too. I had a boyfriend for nearly five years so I think that made people leave me alone.

**CLAIRE** I was a real swot – I took extra Maths classes. I was artistic so I always got A* for Art and Drama and was good at English and History too. Maths and Physics weren't really my bag so I had to work extra hard in those subjects. I used to be called 'Posho' because I spoke well, so it's funny that I'm now playing Jacqui!

**GEMMA** I was really mischievous at nursery and would make stuff up – like telling my mum the teacher had hit me so that she went into the school and really kicked off!

**HOLLIE** I was the biggest chav ever at school!

**JORGIE** Were you the kind of girl I'd have been scared of?

**HOLLIE** Well, I was a geek chav because I was ginger. And I was obsessed with buying a pair of Rockport's which were the in thing to have. They're like a man's boot and cost about £150.

**JORGIE** I wanted some of them!

**HOLLIE** I begged my mum for a pair but she didn't want to let me have any. I got some in the end. I had Paddington Bear glasses too. I was the ugliest child. [Laughs]

**JORGIE** I remember at school you just had to carry all these dictionaries round with you – French, English, Thesaurus and your PE kit! You had to have massive bag!

**HOLLIE** But if you wore your rucksack on your back hanging from both shoulders like you were supposed to, you were called a geek. I remember that the cool thing was to wear a JD sports carrier bag across your body instead.

**JORGIE** [Laughs] I remember that!

**HOLLIE** You'd go into JD Sports on purpose to get something really small like a key ring because that's all you could afford.

**JORGIE** And then you'd ask them if you could have a drawstring bag for it to go in!

**HOLLIE** It was pink and it said 'JD Woman' on it and it was as cool as anything.

**JORGIE** But then I went up to year 11 when I just wore my blazer and the only thing I carried was a pen. I was so cool! [Laughs]

**HOLLIE** I used to try desperately to be popular but I really wasn't accepted because I was too mouthy and ginger. And my nose was too big for my face. Oh and I had my hair in ginger cane rows over to one side! [Others laugh]

## Could you stick up for yourself?

**HOLLIE** Yeah, totally. I was still ugly though!

**JORGIE** You must've had a group of mates who would boast that you were their friend.

**HOLLIE** They did a bit – but what's weird is I'm still friends with most of them and now as they've got older, they're the ones who stand up for themselves and I'm more shy and embarrassed.

## Were any girls jealous of you?

**JORGIE** I've been bullied. I think it was because I got given a solo. One girl made me feel awful and think it should have gone to someone else. I wouldn't make a big deal out of it, but I sort of wished I'd never got given the solo just to ease the tension and so I could go home. Jealousy is the worst thing in the world. I would never be jealous of someone else. All that's important is to think about what you can do, not focus on what other people can do.

**GEMMA** I used to sing in the concerts at school and everyone used to be so nasty to me and I remember talking to my mum about it. She used to say it was jealousy. I didn't believe her at the time but she was right. Like Jorgie said, jealousy is the worst thing in the world.

## Did you enjoy school?

**JORGIE** I absolutely loved school!

**HOLLIE** The bit I liked was that the lads changed so much more than the girls and one day you'd see some guy who'd randomly got really tall and you'd say, 'When did he get good-looking? Where did he come from?'

**CLAIRE** I enjoyed first school more than second. I think when you get older, people's personality traits and cruelty come through more.

**GEMMA** I hated school; I got bullied and didn't have many friends. I'd hang out with my mum all the time – she was like my best friend.

**HOLLIE** I questioned everything at school – I was the most hideous teenager ever.

**JORGIE** In my last year I skived every lesson and just went to PE and Drama. I had to do it because I couldn't face Maths, it killed me. Numbers and me don't work out very well. So I'd pretend I had to help the Year Sevens with PE. Oh, and once me and my mate were sunbathing outside during Spanish!

**HOLLIE** [Laughs] We used to do that but the only part of you that could get any sun was a tiny bit of belly if you rolled your shirt up!

**JORGIE** I know! It was hardly worth it. And the teacher said, 'If you're going to skive, girls, go somewhere we can't actually see you!'

### You had a tough time at school, Gemma. Want to talk about it?

**GEMMA** I never ever fitted in. I was diagnosed as being severely dyslexic and still wasn't reading when I was seven. I remember sitting there with a book next to my teacher at her desk pretending to read, just making noises – but the teacher didn't even notice. My mum obviously saw what was going on so she took me to a private clinic in Wilmslow where they discovered what was wrong. I was put into a really small school and given special tutoring.

### What happened after that?

**GEMMA** I was sent to a bigger school and I came out in a rash all over my body because I was so stressed and hated it that much. I couldn't understand things, I couldn't write them down and I felt so stupid because I couldn't keep up. Oh god, it was awful. The only thing I was good at was music and dancing. I got bullied because of dyslexia, because I didn't fit in with the 'in' crowd, because I sang and I danced. Every day I dreaded going into school. I remember one day

I'd been coming home, walking to the car where my mum was waiting to pick me up, and this lad in the year above tripped me up and poured a can of Coke over my head. My mum jumped out of the car and grabbed hold of him – she went mental. I still remember that now. Mum went berserk. She was always my biggest support! But the worst was being in the bottom set for things because of my dyslexia – people would say, 'You're stupid.' I was quite a confident little girl but when I got to my teens, because I was bullied so much, I lost it. Bullying doesn't just happen at school, either. There are bullies all through life. I'm not very much of a person to take any crap off anyone now. If they try to start bullying me, I will tell them straight. I'm probably a bit too strong now, too much the other way. I won't give people chances. They get one chance and that's it.

## How did it work itself out?

**GEMMA** Eventually I went to a different school where all the teachers were great and then I went to college and retrained at the Manchester School of Acting. I learnt about sight-reading. The more I practised the better I got. But even now, if I'm nervous, I might panic. The first time I read a script in front of other people was horrendous! I was so stuttery and nervous. It was really hard to do at first.

## And how is life now?

**GEMMA** Since coming to *Hollyoaks*, I've found somewhere I fit in. I feel like this is where I found myself. At school I was always the odd one. There was never really a place for me. But I was never a follower either. I would always say what I thought, and I think that's a good thing. I'm the same to this day.

## What advice would you give to anyone else who's dyslexic?

**GEMMA** Don't let it bring you down or beat yourself up about it. People who are dyslexic always seem to have a talent in the arts somewhere so they'll do really well. Dyslexic people are clever – they just can't always put it on paper.

## What do you remember about your teachers?

**GEMMA** My music teacher was really inspiring and because I was so shy and timid he really brought me out of myself – he made me sing in all the concerts he did for the school. I went back to my school for an awards evening recently and the PE teacher was laughing at me because I never used to want to do anything that I had to go outside for – that mucked up my hair.

**CLAIRE** I had loads of great teachers – me and my best mate Amy made up a rap for our physics teacher! We used to have extra lessons like proper geeks. [Laughs]

## Did you go to many parties?

**GEMMA** My mum would have never let me go to any, even if I was invited! She sheltered me so much – but in a way I'm glad because some of the things people used to get up to were awful. Kids are too young to be doing that sort of thing!

**HOLLIE** Our parties were outside – there was this place called the Brook which was next to a forest and we used to sit round this river and get leathered. We used to hide the booze in the trees if any adults came along.

**CLAIRE** I just remember no one wanted to snog me! There were some girls who were snogging away and I was really left out. I wasn't ready for it then though – it all seemed a bit scary to me. I didn't like the taste of alcohol until I was about 18 or 19 either. I remember putting a cigarette to my mouth for the first time and my best mate Amy just said, 'Oh my god, everyone look at Claire!' because I couldn't do it properly. Looking back now I'm so grateful to her because it stopped me ever wanting to touch a cigarette again. We laugh about it now.

**JORGIE** There were loads of house parties. But people's parents would be there as well – my mate Mary's dad once bought us a Smirnoff Ice each to go to a party and after one sip we were hammered! I remember being dead sweaty and hot. I remember trying to get into pubs too. Looking back at pictures of me at that age I don't know what I was thinking: there's no way I passed for 18. How did I think I was going to get away with it? There's a rule now – when you go out, always wear a coat. Older girls don't prance around virtually naked like we used to!

## What's your school report most likely to have said?

**JORGIE** 'She's got a happy personality but sometimes needs to concentrate a bit more rather than chatting.'

**CLAIRE** 'Outstanding' in Drama and Art – and quite good in history too. In fact, I never got a bad report really.

**JEN** 'Jenny's really good and gets on with all the other kids. She could do with a bit more concentration but her grades are good.'

**GEMMA** 'Gemma's really good – she always has a lovely smile on her face and is never naughty.'

## Did you ever get told off?

**GEMMA** No! I was really good, I never even had a detention.

**JEN** I got told off – for chasing around with the boys.

**HOLLIE** I was the one all the boys wanted to play bulldog with. I was such a tit in school. I hate thinking about it actually.

**JORGIE** I wore no knickers on purpose once and the teacher summoned my mum into nursery because of it. She said, 'Your daughter keeps spinning round on the chair and flashing.'

**CLAIRE** I remember this dinner lady screaming at me for standing up and clearing my plate at lunchtime once and it really rocked me.

My parents had never shouted at me or spoken to me in that way and I was so upset. I went to the toilet and just bawled my eyes out for ages. My mum was so angry she phoned up the next day. That's when I realized that people could just be unreasonable.

**HOLLIE** I was always getting told off. Once we had a dancing lesson and we had to take our shoes off but I refused because I hadn't painted my toenails. I wouldn't tell the teacher why, I just refused. I don't really like to conform or get told what to do.

## Were you scared of exams?

**GEMMA** I had the fear of god – having dyslexia didn't help. We had a bit longer to do the exams but it didn't make any difference.

**JORGIE** Exams to me were like the best time because you could see everyone and socialize. You could see the fit boys walking past.

**HOLLIE** I'm quite competitive so I would really want to do well but I just wasn't willing to put the time into it.

**CLAIRE** So scared! I took it all very seriously. But I did get distracted in the Maths exam by a spider crawling across my desk.

## Are you glad you worked hard?

**CLAIRE** Definitely. I think it's important. People might not think that as an actress you need all those other disciplines but you need History for plays, and English for an understanding of language and how to work a script. Geography is another thing. The only subject I'm not convinced about is Maths because I've not needed simultaneous equations yet. But you never know!

## What were your best lessons?

**JORGIE** PE was my favourite! If I forgot my kit I would wear the stuff from lost property just because I didn't want to miss out.

**HOLLIE** Were you always Centre in netball?

**JORGIE** Yeah – how do you know?

**HOLLIE** The little pretty ones are always Centre in netball!

**JEN** I hated PE. I don't think I've ever done a PE lesson!

**HOLLIE** I was in *Grange Hill* during my last year at school and there was this boy who sat at the back of the class and sung the theme tune whenever I walked in. He thought it was the funniest thing.

### Was being in *Grange Hill* seen as cool or were people jealous?

**HOLLIE** Oddly I had a teacher who was jealous. She was horrible to me. I was late into class one day because of being on set and she said, 'Where have you been?' knowing full well that I'd been at *Grange Hill*. I replied that I'd been at work. 'Where do you work?' she demanded. She wanted to embarrass me and make me say it in front of the class. But I refused to be drawn and just said, 'In Liverpool, miss.' The others were shouting, 'Miss, miss! She's on *Grange Hill*, didn't you know?' Then she paused, looked at me and sniffed: 'I had visions of you being a cleaner.'

**JORGIE** That's awful!

**HOLLIE** Then she said, 'I think you're going to have to give up that hobby of yours.' I think she looked down on Drama. I just couldn't make myself interested in Science or Maths – I was into Art, English and Music, so trying to teach me those other subjects was like trying to teach a mouse how to bark.

**CLAIRE** I didn't think acting was an option back then so for ages I wanted to be an art teacher. My whole family can paint and draw so I thought that was what I wanted. I was also a gymnast from four to fourteen. It was pretty intense – I did gymnastics six days a week. It was like a proper job after school each night.

## Did you have a Saturday job?

**CLAIRE** I worked at Miss Selfridge on a Saturday and on a Thursday evening. I thought I was well cool. We got a 25 per cent discount on the clothes – but we had to wear a uniform back then, rather than the clothes in store, which was some horrible red shirt.

**GEMMA** I worked at All Sports in the Trafford Centre on Saturdays and on a Thursday night after college.

**JORGIE** I was a lifeguard – I did nudist nights!

**JEN** You what?!

**JORGIE** I had to look after naked people! There was a night at the swimming pool where I worked specially for naturists.

## Did you have to be naked too?

**JORGIE** No, but I felt silly wearing clothes. They'd all be really confident and come over to me swaggering. They were all shaven too! I found it interesting seeing the women's bodies, though. It was amazing how confident they were even when they were all shapes and sizes. And they were with their kids sometimes, so it was like they were teaching their kids to feel good about their body too. It made me feel much less picky about my own shape after that.

# Drama rama

## " I was a pretty reluctant drama student . . . "

*Hollie-Jay Bowes*

---

### When did you get into acting?

---

**GEMMA** Musical theatre was my passion, but in order to make it I thought I'd have to move to London and I wasn't ready. Besides, my parents couldn't afford to send me to drama school full-time, and I didn't want to live on nothing. So I thought I'd take a couple of years out and earn some money, and ended up working on the Aveda counter in Selfridges, then moved to another job in that industry. It was great having a job to start with – I felt really independent. But then the acting buzz started coming back and I knew I wasn't where I should be.

**HOLLIE** I was a bit of a reluctant drama student – I went to a Saturday class while I was at school and we went to France to do a workshop. And I remember sitting there thinking: this isn't what I want to do. I thought it was too hard. I was a lazy cow and didn't want to do my work and learn my lines. But unbeknown to me I'd got an agent from being there. Someone had come out and spotted me. That's how I ended up getting a part in *Grange Hill*.

**JEN** I did quite a bit of acting when I was at school – my mum enrolled me into a child's agency and my dad really encouraged me to be an actress when he was alive too. I remember the day I got my first acting job when I was 13. My dad picked me up from school and told me there was a message for me to call my agent. The smile on his face said it all. I appeared in *Where The Heart Is* twice and I was in *Emmerdale* and *At Home With The Braithwaites* and did a couple of adverts – one was for Minky cleaning products. But that was all up until I was about 16 – then it started to slow down a bit because I looked quite old for my age.

**JORGIE** I was a hotel entertainer in Greece. We had to talk to families in the daytime and be really cheesy.

**CLAIRE** I was in this local theatre group when I was about 13 and we had people from the National Youth Music Theatre involved in it too, which meant people started noticing us because they were so talented. It was infectious and I just knew I wanted to do it. My mum and dad could see I thrived on it too and they encouraged me. Teachers would say that I had a knack for properly understanding scripts and knowing where to put intonation in the lines. I stopped pursuing my gymnastics soon after that because it was just impossible to do both.

### You did some TV work before *Hollyoaks*, didn't you?

**CLAIRE** I was lucky enough to get quite a few meaty parts. I was in *Waterloo Road* and had to give birth in the classroom. I was playing opposite Angela Griffin, a well-established actress, which was pretty amazing. I guess it was a big deal but I always treated any job just like it was – a job. I did my homework, learnt my lines and I think as long as you do that you can't go wrong.

### What do you remember about your first time on stage?

**CLAIRE** The first proper musical I did was *The Boyfriend*; I played a character called Fay. It was a really big deal for me because there were a lot of other girls who could have got the part over me – I had to sing a solo in it and I hate singing. I can sing in tune but I don't rate myself as a singer. Maybe I'm too much of a perfectionist. I played Auntie Em in *The Wizard of Oz* too – I always seem to play character parts.

**GEMMA** I went through a time where I was so nervous I was nearly sick before I went on stage. But the more I did it, the more I got used to it. I always worried what people thought but I knew I just had to get over it.

**JEN** I didn't do any theatre – I just didn't think that was for me.

**GEMMA** I did a musical called *Goodnight Mr Tom* while I was at school – it was on for about six months and I did it in the evenings. It was brilliant.

## Did you go to drama school?

**CLAIRE** I wanted to be a quality actress and to get a decent agent I knew that I needed to go to drama school. I did B-tech Performing Arts and A level Art then went on to do an acting degree at Guildford School of Acting. I got into drama school through a scholarship. My mum and dad wouldn't have been able to afford to send me otherwise. There were auditions for the scholarship places and I was lucky enough to get a letter through the post saying I'd got in. It was fantastic. It was hard though – I had lots of competition. I was in a hugely talented year. I wasn't the favourite and I wasn't a swot. But when I graduated I was given the acting award for that year – it was really unexpected because I'd never been a main part, but I'd obviously been noticed and it meant a huge amount to me. Especially as my boyfriend dumped me on that day! At the end of your three years in drama school you do a showcase of your work in the hope that an agent will see you and take you on. I did mine in London – it was like a cattle market, everyone competing against each other. I had an allergy attack I was so stressed! It really was tough. But I got an agent who was fantastic.

**GEMMA** After working at Selfridges and then Harvey Nichols I joined a school for TV acting run by Mark Hudson, who's the acting coach at *Hollyoaks*. The fact that I'd done so many musicals was a hindrance to getting any TV work – they don't like it if you're too 'stage' and it goes against you. So I knew I needed more experience and went once or twice a week then wrote off to loads of agents until I got one – then *Hollyoaks* came up.

**JEN** I didn't. I ended up doing a doing a degree in Health and Fitness because the drama degrees just didn't interest me. In my head you could either act or you couldn't – it wasn't something that could be taught. I was really into going to the gym at this point. So I just threw myself into that and then worked in a gym for a couple of years as an instructor there, and then I worked in sales for gym memberships.

## What made you go back into acting?

**JEN** After a while I just thought: come on, try it, Jen, because I'd actually started feeling guilty for not putting what I felt was an alright talent to use. It was a bit like I'd let my mum down too because she'd sent me to so many acting lessons when I was at school and had put her money and time into something she thought I was good at. So I thought I owed it to her as well. I got one of the lads at work to take some pictures of me, handwrote a few CVs and sent them out to agents. A couple came back and were interested and I chose the one I'm still with now.

**CLAIRE** I used to do up houses between acting jobs. Not just a little bit – they needed new roofs and everything. I was a bit of a property developer! I didn't know what I was doing at all at first but I learnt fast. I remember going down to London for auditions and between jobs I'd have someone plastering and rewiring my house. I've sold them all now – but it was good to have another talent, something else to focus on. I've always been known as a bit of a grafter by my mates back home.

## What advice would you give someone who wants to get into acting?

**CLAIRE** My biggest tip is to go to your local library, find a good selection of plays and read as many as you can. If you want to go to drama school most teachers will ask you what plays you've read and you can't just look at them and say, 'I want to be an actress' or 'I want to be famous' – you need to show a passion for it and a genuine interest. They like people to have a knowledge of literature and an understanding of it. Also go to as many local clubs as you can – singing, dancing, acting – it's a bonus if you can do a bit of everything. And one more tip – people watch. I do that all the time. If I'm on a bus I study people's behaviour, the way people walk and talk. It's so helpful when you have to become a character. I don't talk or behave like Jacqui in real life – I based her on someone back home.

**GEMMA** I would say don't put too much pressure on yourself – do what you can do, don't go with the crowd and keep focused. Go for your auditions and be the one who stands out.

# Casting / Characters

**"I based her on the people who used to live near me in Barnsley – they were rough round the edges but salt-of-the-earth types and would speak in a drawl"**
*Claire on Jacqui McQueen*

## Hollyoaks characters

Claire: Jacqui McQueen

Hollie-Jay: Michaela McQueen

Gemma: Carmel Valentine

Jennifer: Mercedes Fisher

Jorgina: Theresa McQueen

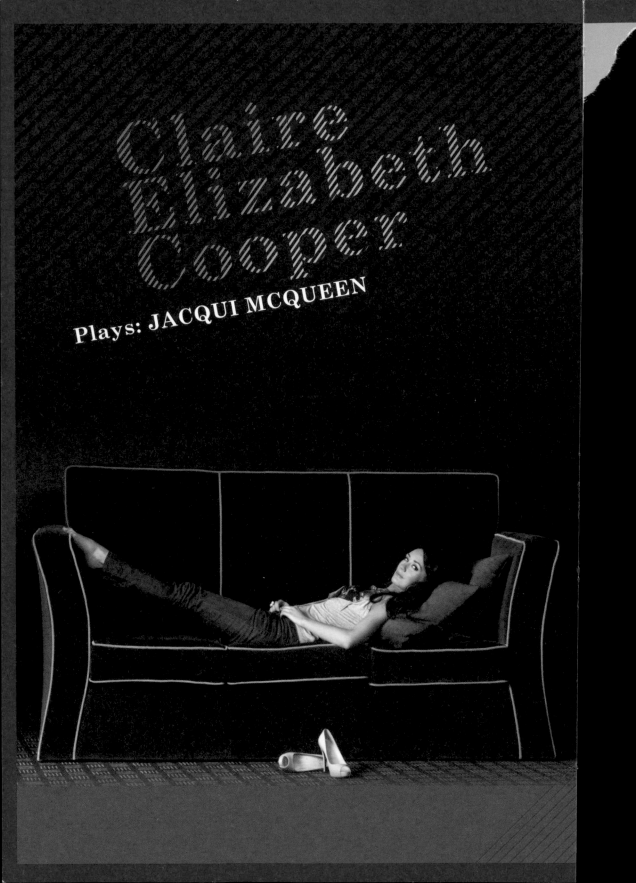

# Claire Elizabeth Cooper

## Plays: JACQUI MCQUEEN

**Birthday:**
It's 26 October. I'm a Scorpio.
I love all that tarot and psychic
stuff, it really interests me. I've
had a few spot-on readings.
Scorpios are supposed to be
passionate, strong-headed,
sensitive and you wouldn't want
to cross them. Which is very true
with me – I'm extremely loyal but
if someone breaks my loyalty
I'm very wary. I don't forget
things; I'm like an elephant.

**Most likely to send a text saying:**
'What you doing?'

**Fave body part:**
I quite like my tummy –
my abs are pretty toned.

**Dislike most about myself:**
I have a horrible habit of bringing
myself down and I worry all
the time, it's a really negative
thing. I'll find something each
day to worry about and it's
annoying because I know I'm
doing it. Sometimes it's genuine
and sometimes it's not.

**Last lie I told:**
I can't lie! I try to tell the truth
even if it hurts people but the only

**Bet you didn't know that . . .**
I was a British Champion
gymnast.

time I might fib is if I need to get
away early or I'm late to meet
someone. The other day I told
my friend I was stuck behind one
of those temporary traffic lights.
That's a familiar trick with me.

**Most embarrassing moment:**
I have loads but there was one
recently where I went to park
my car in a car park, got to the
machine, had my phone in one
hand and money in the other.
The money wouldn't go in
properly – then suddenly I heard
this voice saying, 'Hello?' so I
leant into the machine and said,
'Sorry, I didn't realize I'd pressed
a button to talk to someone,' and
the voice replied, 'Are you OK?'
I said, thank you, and that I was.
There was a queue of people
behind me. Then I heard the voice
again – 'Claire?' – I thought:
how does the machine know my
name? Then I realized it was
coming from my phone. I'd called
my publicist Jane by mistake
and it had been her all along.

**Biggest fashion faux pas:**
I used to wear shell suits all the time. And because I was in the local gym club my top had 'Wakefield' on the back of it. I used to walk round town with it on. Cringe.

**My co-stars would describe me as:**
Odd, fun, genuine and a bit temperamental on occasions.

**Proudest moment:**
When I graduated from Guildford School of Acting I got the Acting Award. I never thought I'd been noticed at drama school – I never had a main part, just character parts – but I obviously had been spotted over all those years. It couldn't have come at a better time either – my long-term boyfriend had just dumped me. Whenever I'm out of work or feeling sad I look at it and it lifts me.

**Favourite flavour cheese:**
Wensleydale.

**Biggest regret:**
Spending far too much money on exes.

**Most expensive thing I've ever bought (apart from car and house):**
A bespoke kingsize luxury bed – that was pricey!

**Top three happy tunes:**
I love anything by Cat Stevens, and Muse's 'Starlight'. Beyoncé's 'Single Ladies' always gets me on the dance floor.

**My friends call me . . .**
Coops.

**Last time I cried:**
Yesterday. I went to Nicole's – who plays my mum, Myra McQueen – and I was questioning where things are in my life. She said, 'Come here, you want a hug, don't you?' and it made me well up.

**What makes me laugh?**
I know it sounds awful but I laugh when people fall over. Not when they hurt themselves – but when someone trips up. People can laugh at me if it happens to me – that's fine too!

**If I want to treat myself . . .**
I go and get a new outfit.

Claire – Hollyoaks Calendar 2010

# in the spotlight

## chapter 2

Must be nice getting your picture taken for magazines, right? But what happens when you're on holiday, sweating in your bikini, squeezing the blackheads from your mate's back only to get on a plane home to discover someone has taken a photo of it? Not so nice. Welcome to the world of the *Hollyoaks* girl – where glamorous studio shoots dripping with personal stylists and make-up artists go hand in hand with sneaky paparazzi waiting in bushes to catch her unawares – and better still get a shot up her skirt.

Here the girls speak about coping with the pressures of fame – the excitement of being on the pages of fashion spreads to the upset of being criticized for looking 'too thin' or dating the wrong sorts of fellas. Being famous means you're also fair game.

# Fame game

## " One magazine made me out to be a weird bunny boiler! "

*Jennifer Metcalfe*

### When did you first realize you were famous?

**CLAIRE** When this woman saw me outside the Mayfair hotel in London recently and said, 'Oh my god, it's Claire Cooper.' It always used to be, 'There's Jacqui!' so it's nice when people know your real name. I still get 'Jacqui!' if people recognize me, though.

**JEN** I don't think of myself as being famous. I honestly don't think I am a 'celebrity'. To me I'm not any different to how I used to be.

**JORGIE** I first thought it when I heard people shout my character name 'Theresa' at me.

**HOLLIE** But what some people don't realize is if there's a big group of them it's a bit intimidating. The other day there was a gang of girls and they shouted, 'Michaela!' but I didn't turn round because there was so many of them. Then I heard them saying, 'Who does she think she is? She thinks she's a celebrity!' and then they followed me!

**JEN** It's nice when people come up to you and are really enthusiastic about *Hollyoaks*. There's a time and a place for it, though. I've been sat in a bar with a friend and she's been upset about something – and someone came over and asked for a photo. The problem is, if I say, 'Do you mind just leaving it today?' they think you're up yourself. They gave us loads of abuse for that, which just wasn't fair.

**HOLLIE** People are very quick to think you're being rude and that you love yourself. I find it really rude when people come over to you if you're eating a meal with your family. I would never have done anything like that.

**JEN** There have been times when me, Gemma and Claire have been out on a Saturday night and if we're being all loud like the McQueens then we're kind of asking for it.

**JORGIE** I found it really weird when we did T4 on the Beach because there were all these people screaming at us! They were banging on the windows of our minibus!

**JEN** The worst time for me was when we did the Clothes Show in Birmingham. There were thousands of people – I felt like Posh Spice walking about!

**CLAIRE** I like it when people have really watched you or read something you've done in a magazine or just taken a genuine interest in you as a person – like the other day a woman came over and said, 'I saw you in *Closer* magazine the other day and you looked lovely, you don't look anything like your character in real life!' I appreciate stuff like that.

## What about when you walk down the street?

**GEMMA** More people notice us the longer we've been in the show. This year it seems to have got much more obvious. Everywhere I go, even if I'm in my tracksuit, with no make-up and a hat on, they still seem to know who I am. But to me that shows the character is popular and the programme's doing well.

**CLAIRE** People just generally look at me oddly and then walk off! I was followed the other day though and wasn't in the mood for it at all – I was going to the shops and this group of kids trailed me to every place I went. I asked if they were alright and having a nice day and they just looked at me blankly and said, 'Yeah.' So I felt an idiot. I thought they'd leave after that but they kept following me!

**HOLLIE** I was really taken aback in the supermarket once when this guy came over to me and said, 'Hollie-Jay Bowes?' He said, 'I just googled your name on my phone because I thought it can't be all that nice when people call you by your character name.' I was actually quite flattered by that!

**GEMMA** My mum loves it when people recognize me! Whenever I'm out with her she says to people, 'Do you want a picture?'

## What's it like having stuff written about you?

**CLAIRE** I like it when papers write something nice, of course! But when they write stuff about your personal life I don't feel very comfortable with it. Saying that, I don't really do so many shoots for the lads' mags so the papers don't pick on me as much as some of the other girls.

**GEMMA** I remember when we joined the show and my first picture got in the paper – I was in the *Daily Star* and it made me think: oh my god, this is actually real! It suddenly hit me that people might know who I was, it was weird.

**JEN** I've probably had the most flack over the years – there were some shots of me on holiday with some of my mates and all the magazines were saying I looked really thin. Looking back, I did look skinny – but the thing with me is that my weight always fluctuates so it certainly wasn't something I'd done on purpose.

## How did it affect you?

**JEN** It was just a bit heavy that all eyes were on me for being someone who was 'dangerously thin'. They were saying you could see my ribs and I looked unhealthy. When people say things like that it's bound to get to you but it was more frustrating to have things written that were untrue. I was eating loads! My mates were laughing when they saw all the articles because they'd been with me and seen me scoffing my face.

## Do people get their facts right about you?

**CLAIRE** Everywhere always gets my age wrong! No magazine has ever got it right. They either put five years on me or take five years off me.

**HOLLIE** That's the danger of Wikipedia!

**CLAIRE** I know because people take that as fact when it's just someone at home who's decided to set up a Wikipedia page about you. But if people think I'm 30 that's fine. But I'm not. [Shrugs]

# Party time

## " When I get drunk I get really drunk "

*Claire Cooper*

---

**Which awards are the most fun?**

---

**JEN** The British Soap Awards are the best because everyone gets to go – it's like a massive soap party where we all let our hair down.

**HOLLIE** Everyone was giddy the year when the McQueens were nominated for Best Family. *Hollyoaks* always gets plenty of nominations. The McQueens have had some fantastic storylines.

**JORGIE** The Soap Awards are good but there's a lot of time waiting for the awards to be announced. I was nervous too the first year I went because I was up for best newcomer and was thinking: if I win, I have no clue what to say. So I was just really worried about that, thinking I could be in serious shit if I had to make a speech. I didn't want to look like a dick. I didn't get the award and in a way I was relieved! Sometimes I think things happen for a reason and that was the case with me because I wouldn't have known what to say.

**GEMMA** I loved the first year better than when I've been since, though. I think they're a bit samey. But I probably say that because in my first year of being in *Hollyoaks* I won Best Comedy Actress, which was amazing. To achieve something like that – and remember that a year before I was working at a make-up counter. It's been the biggest confidence boost and learning curve.

## Who gets the most drunk on a night out?

**GEMMA** Jenny!

**JEN** [Laughs] It depends on the night. I probably get drunk the most often . . .

**CLAIRE** But when I get drunk I get really drunk.

**GEMMA** Jen gets drunk super quickly and I can never understand it because she drinks more than us usually so should be able to handle it better! Once I'm gone, though, that's it, I can get completely hammered. When Jen and me are out together we're a nightmare – we drive everyone a bit insane.

**HOLLIE** I'm a really happy drunk. Although I'm a little bit lairy. If someone annoys me then that's it – and I forget I've got a big mouth when I'm drunk. I'll shout things unnecessarily like, 'Oh god, I need a wee!' when I could just go quietly.

**CLAIRE** Jen always disappears! We'll be out together then I'll look round and she's gone. I'll text her to find out where she is, and she'll be, 'I'm in bed.'

**JEN** [Laughing] The thing is, when I need to leave I need to leave. What about that time we went to Mission?

**CLAIRE** That was a big one.

**JEN** We were on a big night out in Leeds.

**CLAIRE** Till about 4 a.m.

**JEN** It was some of my mates from Leeds, and Claire.

**CLAIRE** I just came on my own!

**JEN** We got drunk because the music was really good – then we went onto this really dirty club and it was the first night I'd worn my leopard-print Louboutins and I was wobbling about all over the place. We got talking to this group of lads, who were really quite fit . . .

**CLAIRE** We were dancing talking . . .

**JEN** And I was dancing and lord knows how I did it but—

**CLAIRE** She had a bottle of Bud in one hand—

**JEN** [Matter of factly] Peroni.

**CLAIRE** OK, Peroni. [Laughs]

**JEN** And I had the bottle in one hand and my watch was on my opposite wrist, and somehow that heel got stuck in the watch and I was just left wobbling in mid-air and fell sideways!!

**CLAIRE** And she threw the drink on me!

**JEN** I got up and was so embarrassed. I thought: I can't stay here now, so I went to the loo and had to take my tights off because I had a ladder all down them. I was thinking: there's no way I can go back out there! But I had to get my phone and bag. So I rushed back and picked them up and mumbled, 'I just need to go back to the toilet again.' Claire said, 'Are you going home?' and I was like, 'No, no, just the toilet.'

**CLAIRE** She does it all the time. Just disappears!

### Is it because you don't like goodbyes?

**JEN** I think I just get to the stage where I want to leave there and then. If you start telling people you're going they might say they want to come too and take ages getting their bags and calling a taxi . . . then I'll have to drop everyone off home first. I just want to go! I only do it if there's a fairly big group though – I wouldn't do it if I was just with one person.

**GEMMA** I remember we went out one night to this gig—

**JEN** Oh yeah, and you had a red dress on like Marilyn Monroe! Gemma was so drunk she fell flat on her face on the floor outside and I fell on top of her! We were wetting ourselves laughing and people were shouting, 'The McQueens!' It looked like a scene from *Hollyoaks*. Claire was being all serious saying, 'Come on now, get up, you're being embarrassing!'

### Do you get guys coming up to you a lot when you're out?

**JEN** I think when there's a big group of us we're a bit loud, to be honest. We scare them off!

**CLAIRE** We're always in our own little bubble.

### Have you ever been really rock'n'roll and trashed hotel rooms?

**JEN** No, I'm the opposite! I'm more likely to tidy a room than to trash it. My hotel rooms look neater when I leave than when I arrived!

# Oooh the Glamour

## " When I have to pull 'sexy faces' I have to pretend it's not me sitting there "

*Jorgie Porter*

---

### What's it like doing shoots for the lads' mags?

**JEN** Way before I was in *Hollyoaks* I remember my ex-boyfriend saying to me, 'Why don't you send your picture into one of the magazines?' You know, when they had those sections where boys would send in shots of their girlfriends?

**GEMMA** The first one I did was a bit embarrassing. The photographer didn't give me any direction, which made me feel a bit of a plonker. It's definitely a learning experience – I've learnt so much about how to do shoots since. The photographer Jeannie Savage is amazing and I always work well with her.

**HOLLIE** I haven't done any lads' mags – I wish I had, actually. But with me I think I'd want them to be a bit different. I haven't got the blonde hair and big boobs or the perfect everything – I'd want to do a shoot where I'm wearing boots and something a bit rocky.

**CLAIRE** I've done a few and I don't mind them but it's not really me. I did this weird lingerie shoot when I first started. They were nice pictures, though, so it was fine. We did the calendar, too, which was fun because all the girls got to participate. I think editorial fashion shoots suit me better than the glamour ones. I haven't got a curvy figure – I've got a sporty body that some men will like but I haven't got massive boobs. That's not me.

**JORGIE** I did a lads' mag. I was so nervous beforehand because I didn't have a clue what they'd look like afterwards – they were telling me to tilt my pelvis in a certain way and tilt my boobs, and I was in a really awkward position and you don't realize how long people stay in that place to get that one shot!

**JEN** It's one of the perks. I always say it's like having several jobs all rolled into one. I feel like I've got the acting, the modelling, and then you do all the personal-appearance side of things where you get to go out and meet everyone. It's really like loads of brilliant jobs at once. And now mine and Claire's new business, the Closet.

## Isn't it embarrassing having to pose in your undies?

**GEMMA** You are self-conscious to start with – but that's why it's important to have a good photographer to make you feel at ease. Because at the end of the day, we're not models, we're actresses.

**JEN** The first shoot I ever did was for the *Daily Star* – popstar pictures. I was a bit more curvy when I first started and I remember thinking: oh my god, I've got to get everything out! It did feel a bit funny but you've just got to go with it. Because if you start being all prudish then the pictures look naff as well.

**JORGIE** For me it's doing the sexy faces! I think I'm used to it now, though – playing Theresa, she's a bit of a sexy-face puller. You have to go into a character, because otherwise you'll cringe.

**JEN** I actually find that if you're a bit hung-over before a shoot it helps you look more sultry!

**CLAIRE** You have to get yourself into a character; as long as the photographer is encouraging you, it's easier. It helps ease your mind once you see the pictures – the light in those sorts of shots is always really flattering.

**JEN** That's the thing; everyone's so brilliant on the shoots that they make you feel comfortable. You have to remember they've done it loads – they've seen worse than you and they've seen better!

## What preparation do you do before a shoot?

**GEMMA** I used to have a quick fix a few weeks before a shoot and be in the gym all the time – but now I keep on top of things a lot more and go to the gym regularly. But I think how I feel about shoots is an age thing – I'm a lot more secure in myself now than I've ever been. I know what's good and what's not and what I can and can't do.

**JORGIE** My preparation is doing my tan, eating a light meal before the photo shoot and then I'll pig out afterwards. I wouldn't bother doing any last-minute sit-ups – what's the point? My belly's my belly; I don't think it would change overnight. Unfortunately! [Laughs] All the lighting is lovely, though. You always look good.

**JEN** I end up having to be in my bra and knickers a fair bit as Mercedes anyway – but the great thing is that on a shoot you know they're going to make you look good whatever. You know they can airbrush you and chop you in half! Whereas on telly you are as you come, which isn't great when you're feeling a bit bloaty or unhappy with your weight.

## What's it like having to answer 'sexy' questions?

**CLAIRE** Lads' magazines will ask really silly questions. I was once asked if I would ever dress up as anyone. I said yes and then it was: 'Would you dress up as a tree?' It just got ridiculous. They also try to get dirty answers out of you but I just play the prude card.

**JEN** They don't bother me at all; I'm quite open so I take them in my stride.

**JORGIE** All the lads' mag questions are really funny to answer, I love them! They ask things like, 'Would you rather have a gibbon as a sidekick or a robot that did things for you?' I said I'd want a gibbon so I could give him the same colour hair as me.

## Do you think there's stigma against girls who do that sort of modelling?

**CLAIRE** There is a stigma without a doubt, but each girl makes her own choices about what she does and I don't think she should be judged. Personally I don't really do those sorts of shoots. I'm comfortable in my own skin but I just don't like this full-on 'sex' thing, it's not for me. I appreciate women who look good in shoots but at the end of the day if a girl does a really, really sexy, raunchy shoot she's made that choice and she has to understand that people might have an opinion about it. But it's still her choice. [Shrugs]

**JEN** There's a stigma – we're all guilty of judging people for it. Us girls sit around looking at pictures in magazines and expressing opinions about them. But it's nothing really; it doesn't matter.

**GEMMA** I'm very strict about what I do now – I always have to be wearing a bra! Everyone I work with knows what I'll do and what I won't do now.

**HOLLIE** Do girls judge them? Yes, I do. I'll admit it. I look at some girls who are out who are all dolled up and clearly want to be on page 3 – but I think it's degrading. But then you look at someone like Katie Price and you have to have ultimate respect for her because she's made a success of herself from working with what she had. It's just the other girls who look like clones of each other I can't stand – and my worst fear is looking like a clone. Which is probably why I dress a little bit differently.

# Fan-dango

## " We didn't realize there were paps hiding in the bushes! "

*Gemma Merna*

### What's it like being followed by the paparazzi?

**GEMMA** I only really get followed when I'm with the girls – I guess it's more obvious then. The first time me and Jen went out in London we laughed so hard because we couldn't understand why there were all these cameras around us – it was ridiculous!

**CLAIRE** I don't give them any reason to follow me. It's not like I'm dating someone famous or I'm doing something provocative. I am quite private, so I think that helps.

**JEN** The paps up in Liverpool are much nicer than the ones in London. We have a good relationship with them. Me and one of the girls were out the other day and she got a phone call from one of them asking, 'Do you mind if we come and get a picture of you?' And because we were not looking our best I said, 'We'd rather you didn't tonight. Is that OK?' And he replied, 'OK, cool, no problem.' It works for them too, though, because it means you don't mind giving them the odd shot another time.

**CLAIRE** London is much worse though . . .

**JEN** I was in London with Gemma and it was madness when we came out of our hotel. They just didn't seem to care about you, it was just about getting the picture – they stood on our feet, clambering all over us. One guy actually fell over trying to get a picture. We wanted to stroll to the restaurant and it was just impossible. We couldn't see because of all the lights, it was horrible.

**GEMMA** We had to hail a cab but the paps were still trying to get shots of us – they were even putting cameras up our skirts. I don't think that's nice. It's like they don't see you as human.

## Is there ever a way of avoiding all that attention if you're famous?

**CLAIRE** Yeah. Look at Beyoncé – you can't get any more famous than someone like her and she manages to keep her private life to herself. I think it's largely because she doesn't talk about it in the papers. I think if you say you don't like the fame and the attention, then you should keep out of it in certain spheres of your life. If you like to exhibit yourself you ask for it more.

## How do you know what poses work on the red carpet?

**CLAIRE** I've learnt that you always look better when you smile. Although I always seem to get caught talking to people, which looks like I'm snarling. Then you see the shot afterwards in the magazines and I'm like: damn!

**GEMMA** I think it looks nicer if you're a bit freer and less 'posed'. But the paps always want 'the back shot' where you look over your shoulder – and it's so embarrassing turning round and posing like that. It makes me cringe when I have to do it because it feels like you're saying, 'Look at me, I love myself.' But the reality is, the shot is just more flattering taken from behind.

**CLAIRE** I pop my right leg and cross it in a little bit over my left leg and then I might put my hand on my hip and possibly look over my shoulder.

**JORGIE** Every time I look at pictures I've got my hand on my hip and my foot splayed out to one side and I think: why do I do that?

## Do you practise in front of the mirror?

**JORGIE** No, it just happens as soon as the flashbulbs go! Maybe I *do* need to practise in the mirror.

**HOLLIE** I need to start because my photos are all awful! I can never do a decent pose. Whenever I try and do one it always comes out strange.

**CLAIRE** I don't practise but I will try on my outfit the night before and make sure it looks alright. I've looked at other people and thought: they look nice.

## Have there been situations where you didn't know you were being papped?

**GEMMA** I find holidays a bit of a bad one because you sometimes don't have a clue they're there – it's worrying because you have no control over what you look like or how you're being captured.

**CLAIRE** Me, Jen and Gemma went to Marbella once. We were at this place called the Buddha Beach Bar and were drinking all day – well, I had juice because I wasn't very well.

**JEN** [Laughing] Oh yes, she had another allergy attack!

**CLAIRE** I have allergies continuously. Jen thinks there's something really wrong with me. When I've got them I'm just so bunged up and want to sneeze all the time. I carry loo roll everywhere.

**GEMMA** Anyway we were there in our bikinis having a laugh, and what we didn't realize was that there were paps hiding behind some bamboo walls taking pictures of us. In the end someone in the hotel spied them and let us know what was happening so we quickly went and put some clothes on.

**CLAIRE** If I'd known sooner I'd have put a bit of lip-gloss on!

**GEMMA** It was such a shock when the pictures were all over the papers as soon as we got back.

**CLAIRE** The worst bit is that when one of the pictures was being taken, Jen had started talking about boobs for some reason – and I grabbed mine. I think I was saying, 'Well, to be honest I haven't really got any,' and that was the picture that went everywhere! I was so embarrassed afterwards. The paper had written something about Jen talking about her voluptuous E cup while it said, 'Claire cups her small B cup.' It was awful!

**GEMMA** The stuff they write always makes me laugh – one magazine said next to the picture, 'Claire wants a boob job', which was ridiculous! I think they'd also put: 'The girls were all celebrating Gemma's engagement', when in fact we'd celebrated it ages ago! The best thing was that in one shot, Jen was squeezing blackheads out of my back because I always get them from the fake tan – and for once they actually wrote something nicer than the truth. It read, 'Aaah, look at the girls rubbing suntan lotion into each other.'

### Do you get much fan mail?

**CLAIRE** We get them in a bulk load, which will take about three or four solid days to go through.

**JEN** That's why I set up a Twitter account recently – it means fans can get in touch with you on that and it's easy to reply.

**CLAIRE** Do they? No one gets in touch with me!

**JEN** I used to hand-write all my letters but it's hard to find time what with all the storylines to learn, and mine and Claire's online boutique to look after.

**CLAIRE** I reply to all my fan mail – unless it's rude or inappropriate.

**HOLLIE** There's a guy who's 31, who always writes asking for a picture of me on a rocking horse! It's weird. You can't encourage it.

## Do you get sent much rude stuff?

**JEN** You get some funny things – like I once got a cheque for a fiver. When I first started the show I was hustling people at pool for money in my storyline and a viewer sent me the money thinking Mercedes was real. I never cashed it.

**CLAIRE** My mum sometimes helps me go through them and puts them in piles for me to answer. I remember there was one really inappropriate one that she tore up before I saw it! People in prison sometimes write to us. Jacqui's been in prison so she can relate to them! Their questions are actually quite interesting and they give you quite heartfelt letters. I only get irritated if someone just sends a postcard that says, 'Sign this', because it's really impersonal. I like the ones when they've taken the time out to say something, even if they can't write very well or are really young.

**JORGIE** I'll go home and make a conscious effort to reply as much as I can – I think it's important. There was one guy who sent me a rap – it was dead cool.

# Gemma Ann Catherine Merna

## Plays: CARMEL VALENTINE

**Birthday:**
06.02.84. I'm a typical Aquarian. They're described as oddballs but they're genuine and will always give you a chance. But beware – if you hurt them that'll be it. You can't cross them. And they're strong and artistic, which is also very me.

**Most likely to send a text saying:**
'Hey babes xx'

**Fave body part:**
My eyes.

**Dislike most about myself:**
I worry a lot and get really stressed.

**Last lie told:**
I honestly don't lie, I don't know how to do it!

**Most embarrassing moment:**
When I went on one of my first dates with Ian [her fiancé]. I got so drunk he had to take me home and I was sat on my toilet naked taking pins out of my hair shouting, 'Ian! Ian!' I felt awful when I woke up the next day – cringeworthy.

**Bet you didn't know that . . .**
I'm a classically trained singer. I did quite a bit of opera and musical theatre in my youth. Oh, and I can do the splits too!

**Biggest fashion faux pas:**
When I was about 16 I wore a pair of gold shiny leggings and thought I was really cool.

**My co-stars would describe me as:**
Genuine, honest and completely nuts when I've had a few too many to drink.

**Proudest moment:**
Winning Best Comedy Actress at the Soap Awards. It was the year I'd joined and was unbelievable. An incredible feeling. I've got it in my cinema room in my house [*She has a cinema room?!*] alongside photos of me with the girls on set.

**Favourite flavour cheese:**
Brie. Love it.

**Biggest regret:**
I haven't got any. I don't regret anything I've done – I've

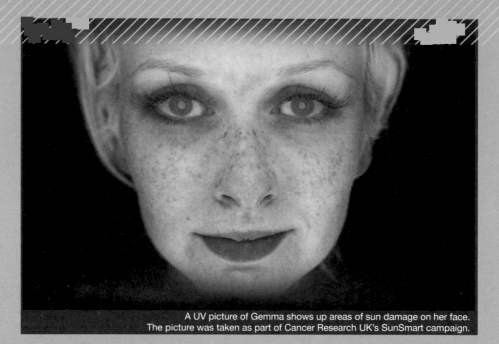

A UV picture of Gemma shows up areas of sun damage on her face. The picture was taken as part of Cancer Research UK's SunSmart campaign.

learnt something from all my mistakes, which I believe can only ever be a good thing.

**Most expensive thing I've ever bought (apart from car and house):**
My Cartier watch – it cost me £3,500.

**Top three happy tunes:**
'Young Hearts Run Free' by Candi Staton, 'New York' by Alicia Keys and 'Girls Just Want To Have Fun' by Cindy Lauper.

**My friends call me . . .**
If anyone calls me anything it's Gem or Gem Gems, or Merna. I get called that a lot at work! 'Oi, Merna, over here!'

**Last time I cried:**
I cry every day! This morning I was watching an interview with the MP John Prescott's wife about how she had to give her son up for adoption when she was 16 and that made me blub. Most things on TV have an effect on me to be honest, I'm a nightmare! [Laughs]

**What makes me laugh:**
Jenny Metcalfe – she's just funny. And she's always burping.

**If I want to treat myself . . .**
I'll go and have a massage, a facial and get my nails done.

Gemma and Jennifer – Hollyoaks Calendar 2010

style secrets

chapter 3

Skimpy clothes? Check. Flashing the flesh? Check. Filming scenes in the – brrrr – freezing-cold winter while having to pretend it's summertime? Check.

One of the many indulgences of *Hollyoaks* is that it acts as an onscreen style advisor – the *Hollyoaks* girls get to prance about in the latest looks from Topshop and co before they hit the rails, giving us the added joy of watching a walking wardrobe. But for the actresses on set, the reality isn't always as glam as it looks. Here they reveal the secrets of how they desperately try to keep warm on set (bet you didn't know the McQueen girls have a hot-water bottle up their skirts most of the time, did you?) and what they really look like when they plonk themselves in the make-up chair first thing in the morning. We also raid the closets of the actresses themselves as they confess to their shopping obsessions, how much money they splurge on designer gear and what it's like to go out to a celebrity party thinking you've scrubbed up well then having your outfit slated in celebrity magazines. From their dodgiest ever fashion mistakes to tips on dressing for your shape – there is no style stone unturned.

# Inside my wardrobe

## " I have outfits in three different sizes because my body weight fluctuates so much "

*Jennifer Metcalfe*

---

**Is working on Hollyoaks as glamorous as it looks?**

---

**CLAIRE** [Laughs] Not for me! Playing Jacqui means I look like a chav every day!

**JORGIE** With the early mornings we have – there's nothing glamorous! People would be in shock if they saw me when I first plonked myself in the make-up chair in the mornings. I'm practically asleep for the first 20 minutes when I get in! Theresa wears lots of make-up. I usually doze while I'm having my hair done, then towards the end I'll start to wake up and join in the conversation.

**JEN** Not at all! Everyone comes rolling in wearing their pyjamas with bed hair. I'm the first one in the chair for hair and make-up.

**HOLLIE** I wouldn't say it was glamorous, I'd say it was tiring. You've got to remember us girls wear skimpy nothings all day and it's freezing – all we have under our skirts are hot-water bottles!

**" People would be in shock if they saw me when I first plonked myself in the make-up chair in the mornings "**

**JORGIE** I don't know what we'd do without that invention.

**CLAIRE** I guess in terms of going to events and stuff you could say the show's glam, though. I have an interest in fashion and know exactly what I like. We get to dress up and go out a lot, which is nice. And in a way at those times it's a bonus that I look the way I do on the show because there's always plenty of room for improvement! People sometimes can't believe who I am when they meet me.

## How would you describe your style?

**JEN** I dress according to how big my body feels. I have about three different sizes in my wardrobe because I fluctuate in size so much – but that's just me. It depends what sort of mood I'm feeling in as to what I wear, which means that most of the time the result is that it's just thrown together! I customize everything I buy to make it that bit different each time – take it up a couple of inches, make it tighter at the waist or put a belt on it. Generally my most 'me' outfit would be a big woolly hat and sweat pants – that's what I wear into work. But sometimes I'll go more sophisticated and sexy and other times it'll just be jeans and a vest.

**CLAIRE** I just wear comfy stuff too, usually. I live in joggers and Ugg boots and hats – I feel really happy in my own skin. When I go out my style is a bit more eclectic. I don't follow trends but I can appreciate what's going on in fashion. I just tend to go with the flow and wear what I like. I would probably say I'm more bohemian.

**JEN** You often say you're bohemian, what do you mean?

**CLAIRE** I guess I mean I like having my own style; I don't go for obvious labels by designers. I layer things up; I don't have a specific way. I have things in my wardrobe that I've had for 12 years!

**JORGIE** I try to keep things simple – I hate things that are too fussy. I wear nudey tones and browns. Nothing too bright.

**HOLLIE** I'd describe my style as a mish-mash. I rarely wear the same combination of outfit twice – mainly because I can't remember what I've put together!

**GEMMA** I'm different every day. Most of the time when I'm at home I'm kicking about in my tracksuit. Or if I go out in the day I'll wear jeans and Ugg boots and then if I go out at night I'll wear a pencil skirt or a dress. I like things that are quite fitted and sophisticated and don't have too much on show.

### Are there any celebs whose wardrobe you'd like to raid?

**CLAIRE** Natalie Portman always looks lovely and classic. But then you have someone like Alison Goldfrapp who completely does her own thing and I kind of like that combination of the two. Not that I'd go out with a peacock tail but I admire that.

**JEN** I don't really watch telly or read magazines so I don't know who my inspiration is. [Laughs] It's important to be yourself. I love looking at other people's outfits but, ultimately, I wear what I think looks good.

**GEMMA** I love Sarah Jessica Parker. I think everything about how she looks and acts is great. She always looks amazing. Another one is Eva Mendes because she's quite curvy and always looks stunning.

**JORGIE** The Olsen twins. I like their blazers and jewellery – they were the first to wear simple casual T-shirts even if they were going somewhere that should be posh. I like Nicole Richie's style too. And Megan Fox is dead cool. She can put on a plain T-shirt and a pair of jeans and still manage to make them look really sexy.

**HOLLIE** Lady Gaga! She's my world.

### Would you wear a lobster on your head?

**HOLLIE** I'd wear a fish on my head, yeah – why not?!

> **I'm the first one in the make-up chair for hair and make-up every morning and I'm there for at least an hour** *Jennifer*

## What couldn't you live without?

**JORGIE** At the moment I'm loving nude heels. I've been pictured in them a lot but I still love them. And leggings. I used to slate everyone for their leggings. I'm only a recent convert but now I can't do without them.

**GEMMA** I wouldn't be able to live without my gorgeous designer shoes and handbags.

**JEN** I would have said my gold Jimmy Choo shoes but I lost them! I went to St Tropez and my feet were killing me so I took them off and never saw them again. I'm gutted because they went with everything. Or black tights! When I'm not feeling very good about myself they're a must because they disguise a lot.

**CLAIRE** There's a cream crocheted woolly hat I've got that I bought in H&M. I wear it all the time at the moment. It covers up my hair on my way home after it's been scraped back for Jacqui. I've got a scarf to match that I'm pretty attached to as well.

**HOLLIE** I'm all about skirts. I don't wear trousers. But if there was one item I couldn't live without it would be vest tops – you need one for every occasion, don't you? Casual, going out, dressy, glam.

## What's your favourite shop?

**HOLLIE** Topshop. If I could be sponsored by anyone in the whole wide world it would be them.

**JORGIE** I like Topshop and All Saints. I love the boutique section in Topshop because they do loads of pale, floaty dresses, which I'm really into at the moment.

**GEMMA** For me it's Zara. Everything fits me perfectly in there and looks nice and classic. It's sleek and sexy – even the trousers are really nice.

**CLAIRE** I love online shopping. My favourite sites are ASOS.com and net-a-porter.com – but I also have a browse on other shop websites so I know what to look for when I'm in town. I'm so into shopping online that Jen and I have set up our own site along with Leah who used to play our sister Tina in *Hollyoaks*.

**JEN** Yes, that's my new favourite shop because we don't need to go anywhere else now! I can wear all the dresses from there. Topshop is great.

**CLAIRE** Our website is called the Closet in Liverpool. It's like a VIP online site for people to be able to buy or borrow dresses that celebs have worn.

### Where did that idea spring from?

**JEN** We were round at Claire's one night and she was talking about how she'd love to set up a shop – there's one called Cricket in Liverpool that everyone goes to up north – and I said, 'You know what would be good? If I could get rid of some of my dresses.' I am such a shopaholic – I have about £20,000 worth of dresses.

### Are you the sort of person who wears clothes and then gets bored?

**JEN** The problem is, working in this business, you can't really wear them again even if you wanted to because you end up getting papped! So I told Claire I wanted to do a rail where I could sell all mine.

**CLAIRE** And then it developed and we thought it would be nice to give other girls the opportunity to wear some incredible dresses. So we're trying to raise money for Christie, the cancer charity, in the process. We've also had some fantastic donations from other people. Britney Spears heard about it and she's donated two dresses, as has Alicia Keys, and Cheryl Cole donated a dress she was wearing on the front cover of *Heat* magazine a while back.

**GEMMA** When I was younger I used to buy an outfit and love it so much that I'd wear it three days in a row! Then I'd never want to wear it again. I'm not that bad any more – I think I have more clothes now. If I'm fed up of something I'll put it away for a while and then rediscover it and put it with something else.

**JORGIE** Sometimes I'll go out shopping and change my outfit as I'm shopping – like if I buy a T-shirt I'll think: I like that, I'm going to wear it now! I will wear stuff more than once though – it depends who I've been out with. If I like it and feel good in it I'll want to wear it again.

## What's your shopping weakness?

**CLAIRE** I always get little underwear sets from Topshop and little bits and bobs like that. I'm not one of these girls who has to have expensive stuff but I do like to buy nice things and feel a bit treated. I like dresses too – I'm not arsed about shoes and bags. In fact it's a hassle to have to go and get myself shoes sometimes.

**JORGIE** I have got a bit of a thing for handbags. I'm not allowed to buy them – I have got a few designer ones and have banned myself from getting any more! And at the moment it's lace tops and dresses. I'm going overboard with it and I can't wear them all at once so I don't know what I'm doing!

**JEN** Designer!

**HOLLIE** Alexander McQueen scarves and high-waisted skirts and belts. I have two big bags full of waist belts.

**JEN** For me it's statement pairs of Louboutins. I can't resist them. I think I've got about nine or ten. I love them.

**GEMMA** I always think it doesn't matter what you're wearing as long as you put a good pair of designer shoes with it, or a nice bag, then you're sorted. I've always loved shoes. I think I've probably got about 50 pairs.

## Do you spend a lot on clothes?

**CLAIRE** I bought a beautiful black cashmere Jasmine Di Milo coat which cost me about £1000 but I hardly ever wear it because I keep thinking I need to save it for nice events like opera or the ballet. I just like to touch it!

**JEN** Yes! If I stopped spending money on clothes I'd probably be rich. I spend a fortune. I'm not a bag person though.

**JORGIE** I've banned myself from buying handbags!

**GEMMA** I love them too. They were my obsession but I'm trying not to buy too many things at the moment because I've got a house to build. It's funny when you start becoming an adult and have serious things to spend your money on! You can't go out and buy nice shoes and bags as much as you used to when you had no responsibility.

**HOLLIE** I spend far too much on clothes. I've got my room, which has a wardrobe in, and then the room next door, which has three rails of clothes!

**JEN** If it's a really special pair of shoes I'll buy them and not care how much they are. But really it's dresses that are my downfall – I have loads and spend a fortune on them.

**HOLLIE** I bought a Chloe dress for £980 – it was for an awards ceremony. It's white and looks like it has paint splattered all over it. I'd like to auction it because it was so expensive, but I look at it and say, 'I can't get rid of you!'

**JEN** Mixing designer with high street is always good. Even though I like to spend money on skirts and dresses – I wore a black Hervé Léger skirt to the TRIC awards once and teamed it with a dress from Wallis that I had customized to make it into a top. If you get something classic it will last you for ages and go with loads of other stuff.

## Do you get many freebies?

**JEN** Not really.

**CLAIRE** [Sighs] You get more than me!

**JEN** Do I? I don't think I do. Oh, I got some free Ugg boots not long ago – that was nice.

**HOLLIE** We're lucky – we do get a few freebies. We get hair products sent to work, which is nice. I really like a designer called Rare – the stuff is punky, racy and meshy, which is very me.

**JORGIE** Jammy dodgers! I mentioned them in a magazine once and got loads sent to me in all shapes and sizes! And at T4 on the Beach there was this tent you could go into and just loads of stalls with people giving out free things – trainers, T-shirts and creams. But the people working there know that you get them free and make you feel a bit cheeky if you take too much!

## What state is your actual wardrobe in?

**HOLLIE** I'm definitely a hoarder – my wardrobe is huge and full of things I've owned since I was 15.

**JORGIE** Me and my boyfriend Tom have moved into a new flat, so there's a whole room where all my clothes are piled up over this ironing board and all over the place.

**CLAIRE** I'm not organized at all! I had my tarot cards read once and they said that my grandma was telling me I needed to tidy my wardrobe. I always think: I must tidy my room, and then I get bored halfway through and start putting jumpers in with T-shirts and chucking things everywhere. But I'm lucky in that it is like a 'walk-in' wardrobe. It's just not quite as neat as it could be.

**JEN** I've got three double rooms in my house and still don't think I've got enough room! Melissa who plays Loretta in *Hollyoaks* is living with me at the moment, so I've got all my casual stuff in my room in a big wardrobe with all my gym stuff in drawers. And then I've got a separate wardrobe in my spare room, which has all my dresses and going-out stuff. My shoes are a bit of a mess and it's my own fault because I threw all the boxes away because I didn't like the clutter—

**CLAIRE** That's her OCD kicking in!

**JEN** [Laughs] I know! I'm such a clutter freak. But now I wish I'd kept all the boxes because it would be so much easier to know where they all were. I need to see if I can buy some boxes now!

**GEMMA** I'm in the process of moving house so at the moment everything's in boxes but I'm going to get a nice slanted shoe rack on the wall so you can see everything in front of you. I want a walk-in wardrobe like Carrie has in *Sex And The City*.

**Like a walk-in wardrobe where you can't see anything when you walk in!**

**JORGIE** Like a walk-in floor!

# Steal her style

## " I used to love leopard print but Jacqui has ruined that trend for me now "

*Claire Cooper*

---

**How would you describe your character's style?**

---

**JEN** Mercedes' clothes could be a lot better but then they could be a lot worse as well – I mean she's a proper trollop, isn't she? But I don't get forced to wear stuff I feel uncomfortable in – our wardrobe department is fab.

**CLAIRE** I think Jacqui dresses hideously! My ideal Jacqui outfit would be PVC boots, a mini skirt and a hoodie. I like her in loads of chain jewellery and hideous make-up. I think she owns every bit of leopard and zebra print there is.

**HOLLIE** At the minute Michaela's having a bit of a revamp. Her original style was with the hair bows, which I personally love – but that's because I gave them to her! My mum wanted a designer scarf for Christmas and me and my brother couldn't find the one she wanted so we tracked it down on eBay. But it turned out to be a short one and she'd wanted a long one – so I ended up buying her a new one and just shoving this one round my head and wearing it as a bow because I didn't know what else to do with it. And it stuck!

**GEMMA** I love Carmel's clothes – they're so funny. It's great when you see a really good outfit that you're wearing that day. The only problem is that it's so cold all the time because you're wearing next to nothing! She's very young for her age, they're always clashing – lots of pinks and bright colours. I guess they represent how happy she always is.

**JORGIE** Theresa is fun and feminine, she wears nice clothes actually – I'm the lucky one out of the McQueens! I love them because they're really different to the things I wear outside of work. I'm more into neutral colours and comfy cardigans. We're all used to filming scenes in the freezing cold now though – but it can be unbearable sometimes. I wish Theresa would learn to cover up a bit more! The worst thing is that because we work so far ahead it means we're filming summer stuff when it's winter, which means even more skimpy clothes!

## Have you ever been tempted to steal any of your character's clothes?

**CLAIRE** Never! I used to quite like leopard print but Jacqui's ruined that trend for me now. If I put it on people automatically associate me with her so I have to be quite careful what I wear. I did once borrow a belt that belonged to Mercedes, though – it's one of the nicer pieces in her wardrobe. If I went out as Jacqui people would run a mile – I'd never get a snog! Mind you, I don't anyway. [Laughs]

**JORGIE** There are a few dresses and jackets of Theresa's that I'd really like, to be honest. I wouldn't dare steal them, though!

**JEN** I donated one of my dresses to Mercedes – so it was the other way round! I've given her a few things actually. Stuff I've worn when I was younger. She has my hand-me-downs! But as for her things, I can't think of one item I'd like to borrow. [Laughs]

**GEMMA** I borrowed one thing – it was a white sequinned mini skirt that was a copy of a Chloe skirt. I wore it out one night with a black top and it was lovely. I did give it back afterwards, though – the costume department's lovely with me!

## Any wardrobe malfunctions on set?

**JEN** My boobs are always falling out on camera! They're not huge but they seem to like getting noticed. [Laughs] I did a scene once where I had to take my top off but leave my bra on. But when I took my top off my boobs fell out! I didn't get embarrassed though – I just tucked them back in. We all get wardrobe malfunctions.

**JORGIE** I had some jeans that were way too tight but I was too shy to say I didn't really like them; I'm not really badass enough. They were dead tight round the waistband and then the arse was near my ankles. [Laughs] Sometimes you're allowed to keep your coat on if you feel really rubbish though.

**JEN** Mercedes has to wear really tight outfits, which is unfortunate for me. A skimpy dress is the last thing I want to wear – especially after a naughty weekend of takeaways and wine.

# Shape up

## " I sometimes wish my boobies filled my tops up more! "

*Jorgie Porter*

### How have you learned to dress for your shape?

**JEN** With me, as long as I'm happy and my clothes fit, I don't care if I lose or gain a stone. I'm usually about an 8. I find fitted clothes work best for my figure. If you try and hide your curves or cover them up you can look insecure. Embrace it I say!

**CLAIRE** I've learnt that you shouldn't wear leggings with a short top – the leggings can pinch round your crotch, which isn't nice. I know what my body suits and I am quite lucky in that I suit a lot of shapes, which means I can get away with most things. But I don't like bustier-type tops on me because if you haven't got massive boobs, it looks like you're trying too hard to create a cleavage when you haven't got one naturally. What suits me much better is a little blouse with a camisole underneath. That actually gives me a better shape.

**GEMMA** I think when you've got big boobs like I have it's important to wear things that are fitted otherwise you can look top-heavy. Baggy tops are a no-no. I've got an hourglass figure so I think it's better to show it. People say it's a bad idea to wear high necklines when you have a big chest, which is true, but if you wear a tight top it's OK. Like I've got a polo neck that's made out of stretchy material and that's nice because it's skintight to my body. But loose-fitting high-necked shirts can make you look really frumpy.

**JEN** I have got a really small waist and a big booty which means I can't wear certain things because I look like a sack. My worst nightmare would be a rounded neck and stubs for sleeves. Or those cute mini dresses that are a bit tent-shaped. They look awful on me. The key with me is showing off my shape, not hiding it.

**HOLLIE** I've got big legs so if I wear a high-waisted skirt it'll accentuate my waist and won't make my legs look as big. From the knee down my legs are quite skinny – it's from the knee up that they're wrong.

**JORGIE** I don't really go in at the waist – I'm very straight up, straight down – so I've learnt to wear waist belts to nip myself in. I never used to know that's what you should do – I would always wear jeans and a baggy jumper. I wear heels a lot more now too, even casually. I'm 5 foot 3 so heels make me look slimmer.

## What body parts do you have an issue with in clothes?

**JEN** I've got a thing about my arms! I always look at pictures and think my arm looks proper chunky. The other night I was getting ready to go out and put this bag on and said to Leah, [who played Tina McQueen] 'My arms are putting me off my bag' – we were laughing for ages after that.

**HOLLIE** I went through a stage of wearing leggings and a short top – and that was not flattering for my behind!

**JORGIE** My belly, that's the bit I'm most conscious of. Sometimes my boobies too – they're not that big and can't always fill the top I'm wearing so I think: gutted.

## What's the best fashion tip you can share?

**JEN** Don't wear anything straight off the hanger. Do something to make it a bit different, even if it's just rolling the sleeves up, wearing a belt, or taking a few inches off the bottom. I'm quite handy with a needle and thread – I can do wonders!

**GEMMA** Just always be comfortable and dress for your figure. Don't try and be anything you're not or think you need to be dead trendy when it might not suit your shape. Be you.

## Any beauty must-dos?

**JORGIE** Mascara is a must – I always let one coat dry and add more. Always moisturize – do it as soon as you get out of the shower as your skin absorbs better. Don't leave your nail polish on too long as it can stain your nails.

**HOLLIE** If you're going out and you have hardly any make-up then make sure your eyes are defined: you've got concealer on and some mascara. That's all you need. You can pinch your cheeks when you're out and that makes you look like you have blusher on.

**JEN** Look after your skin and drink loads of water.

**GEMMA** Water's really important. I would add to that exercise, lots of sleep and only use really good beauty products. I'm a big fan of Armani foundation and Chanel and Dermalogica for the skin.

# What were we thinking?

## " I went to the Soap Awards with a bag in the shape of a watering can "

*Hollie-Jay Bowes*

---

**What outfits have you worn out that you've hated afterwards?**

---

**CLAIRE** Someone designed me a dress for the first Soap Awards I went to and I didn't like it. It just wasn't right for me. I think it was because I'd only just started at *Hollyoaks* and was too easily swayed by what people thought I should wear. I was annoyed with myself afterwards because I should've known to stick with my instincts. Now I've learnt and am very particular!

**JORGIE** There are some pictures I've seen in magazines and I'll think: my belly was a bit big there, maybe I should've worn support pants! There was one picture where I'm in a grey dress, I've got red shoes on and my hair in a pony tail and I think my belly looks like a potbelly. I was papped going out to Panacea.

**HOLLIE** To be honest I think every person gets it wrong when they go to their first awards show – because you're trying too hard. I was young when I started and I went really over the top. I wore a black and purple dress but when I look back on it I think it just wasn't my style at all. The Chloe dress I bought for the Soap Awards was very nice at the time, but then I did go and team it with a watering-can bag!

## Er, you what?!

**HOLLIE** A bag that's the shape of a watering can! But the whole thing wasn't very me. I'm doing Topshop now.

## Which outfits have you been chuffed with afterwards?

**CLAIRE** I wore a Jasmine Di Milo nude sequinned dress to a recent Soap Awards and I loved the whole look, and another dress by her which was long and black that I wore to the National Television Awards – my hair was down and curly and I thought that looked good afterwards. It's not always about looking über dressed up though – there's a picture I've got on my phone taken when I was out at a little do in Manchester and I like how I look in the picture. I look so at ease and comfortable with myself, I've got jeans on, a little jacket and an Alexander McQueen scarf. I prefer that look on me to super smart, if I'm honest.

**JEN** I really liked my gold Hervé Léger dress. Generally I think I get it quite right – and if no one else thinks so it's tough because I like the way I dress. There have been a couple of times where I might think: I don't look too cracking there, but clearly on the night I felt great otherwise I wouldn't have worn it. And if no one agrees with me, I think, so what?

## How do you avoid turning up in the same dress as another celeb?

**GEMMA** I find it hilarious that when there's an awards ceremony coming up you always see people from our show and *Corrie* running around Harvey Nicks trying to find a dress! There's a personal shopper there so if I buy anything she'll make sure the others know.

**JORGIE** If it happened to me I'd think: whoa! Gutted! But hopefully I'd always dress my outfit up differently to any other celebs so it would be OK.

**CLAIRE** I guess just by speaking to the designers and finding out if anyone else has expressed an interest. Or wearing something that no one else will want!

**HOLLIE** The tip is not to wear a freebie that could've been sent to someone else. It happened to me once – we were at David Guest's party and about four of us were wearing the same Karen Millen shoes. They were orange with a black bow and a big diamond on the front. They're not very me when I look back on them now but they really suited what I was wearing, even if they did pain my feet badly. Gemma Atkinson who used to be in *Hollyoaks* was there and she was wearing them too.

**JEN** I don't worry about it. If you look your best in that outfit then it doesn't matter. If someone else has the same dress, chances are they will have styled it differently. It doesn't matter, if you're comfy.

## What's it like to have outfits slated in magazines?

**CLAIRE** It's often more the faces I'm pulling that bother me! Or there was a picture in one magazine where I'm wearing a red asymmetric couture dress for my birthday – it should've looked nice but I don't know what I'd done with my face. My make-up was all over the place – I think I'd gone a bit overboard on the glitter.

**HOLLIE** There was a picture of me in *Closer* magazine and I look awful – it's like I've got a lollipop head! The angle of it makes me look like a horse. I don't think that's so much the clothes as me looking weird. But most of the time I am happy with my fashion sense. I don't have many regrets.

**CLAIRE** I've done fashion shoots in magazines before and sometimes I'm the one that slates them a bit afterwards – more because I don't think some of them make the most of what they've got. People are always trying to make me look dead natural when I can actually scrub up really well! One or two shoots have made me feel really good in them but more often than not they get it wrong with me. And it's frustrating.

**JEN** There was one recently actually – it was on the front of *More* magazine. I honestly didn't look that bad when I was going into the party! I liked the outfit – it was this camisole top and culottes. But the pictures they've got are shocking. I look all sweaty and disgusting.

**GEMMA** It bugs me the way magazines write about what you've worn to something – they'll put a thumbs down next to you or they'll compare you to someone else. But most of the time mags don't favour the *Hollyoaks* girls.

# When we were young

## " I was obsessed with wearing top-to-toe polka dots "

*Jennifer Metcalfe*

### What clothes did you wear when you were younger?

**CLAIRE** I was surgically attached to my shell suits most of the time. Apart from that I wore a lot of leggings, but they didn't have quite the same look as they do today – they were all baggy round the knees. And I wore clothes that my brother might have worn – like a big baggy check shirt from a man's shop. I also had some red jeans and a polo neck. There was this shop called Sweater Shop which we were all obsessed with when I was about 13–14. You'd have a polo neck with 'Sweater Shop' on it and a stripy knitted jumper over the top. Everyone wore them. Oh and I went through a stage of wearing this huge Oasis T-shirt and cycling shorts for a while. [Grimaces]

**HOLLIE** I wore trackies and denim jackets. I had an Adidas tracksuit that gathered at the bottom, brown Rockport boots and a glittery denim jacket with a top on underneath that said, 'I'm a bitch!' Oh my god! Cringe! I gelled my hair at the back too and had a couple of little curls showing at the front.

**JEN** Aside from my polka-dot obsession, which was standard to me, when I was about 12 I also went through a habit of wearing lumberjack shirts. And I had a big baggy orange shirt that was meant for a man. I loved it.

**GEMMA** I was a terrible dresser when I was younger. I was a bit of an extrovert so I'd go out on a Saturday daytime in a skirt and matching long jacket just to walk round Manchester with my mum. I thought I looked great but I must've looked like some 14-year-old businesswoman! People would look at me as if to say, 'What the hell is she so dolled up for?' I used to wear loads of hats too.

**JEN** I need to see photographic evidence of this!

**GEMMA** I haven't got any photos now – I destroyed them all. [Laughs]

**JORGIE** I used to wear patterned leggings – but that was when they really weren't cool. They were all baggy around the crotch. I've also got a picture where everyone else is in their school uniform and for some reason I'm in big multi-coloured dungarees and a pink jumper with a purple and turquoise roll-neck. I asked my mum about it recently and she said, 'I didn't have any choice in what you looked like, you used to dress yourself.' Sometimes I'd wear denim with denim. Oh, and I used to have these shoes that squeaked when I walked. They had a little mouse face on.

**Oh, you mean they were actually meant to squeak!?**

**JEN** That's hilarious!

**JORGIE** I loved them. They were my special mice shoes.

# JORGIE PORTER

**DAYWEAR:**

My rule generally is to put something busy with something neutral. This lace jacket is from Topshop. I got it because it was the first one out and I wanted it before everyone else. My pink frilly vest is from Topshop; it's cute because you can wear it with shorts or dress it up for a night out. These leggings are from Topshop and my sandals are from Topshop! I got the sandals as soon as we went into summer because I'd been wearing my Ugg boots all winter and I was sweating. I'd wear this outfit for a pub lunch, shopping or meeting my friends.

## EVENING WEAR:

This cream dress is from Topshop – I love cream at the moment. The shoes are Louboutin. So I've got a £30 dress and a £400 pair of shoes. I can't dance in them, though. I told my boyfriend if he got me some Louboutins I'd do anything he wanted!

# CLAIRE COOPER

**DAYWEAR:**

The jeans are from AllSaints, the vest and scarf are from Topshop. I wear scarves quite a lot – if you've got fake-tan marks they're good for covering up the blemishes! They also dress up an outfit. I'd wear that outfit shopping, going to work or for a few drinks in a local pub. That's my comfy style.

### EVENING WEAR:

The nude Jasmine Di Milo dress is the one I wore to the soap awards but I can't wear it much any more because all the sequins attach themselves to each other. The black dress is by Balenciaga; people can rent them from our shop, the Closet.

# HOLLIE-JAY BOWES

**DAYWEAR:**

This is my casual outfit and it's head-to-toe Topshop. My tights are laddered but that's because I refuse to throw them away for a little hole – they cost about £8 a pair and it's a waste! I wouldn't ever ladder a pair of tights deliberately but I will continue wearing them if they've got ladders.

**EVENING WEAR:**

My dress is from
Topshop and I had it
altered at the front so it's
shorter than at the back.
My shoes cost about £20
from a shop in Oldham

# JENNIFER METCALFE

**DAYWEAR:**

With me it's one extreme or the other. I'm either really casual or dressed up to the nines. These are pyjama bottoms from Dolce & Gabbana and I could wear them all the time. They've got buttons for your willy if you're a man. The top is from AllSaints and is nice and loose and baggy.

## EVENING WEAR:

Gold Louboutins that I won from an ex-boyfriend when I beat him at bowling. I get them in a right state, though. You'd never realize how expensive they are from the mess they're in after a night out. The dress is from Topshop. I like to mix designer and high street. If you just wear high street you can look like everyone else, and if you wear all designer you can look like an over-the-top WAG.

# GEMMA MERNA

**DAYWEAR:**
True Religion jeans I bought
in Vegas, the wedges are from
Office, the top is Gap and
the grey jacket is from Zara.
I'd wear this outfit for a nice
lunch with Ian or the girls.

**EVENING WEAR:**
A leopard-print Agent Provocateur all-in-one body and a French Connection pencil skirt. It's a really lovely outfit and perfect for a night out. The shoes are Miu Miu – I got them for my birthday about two years ago. I'm obsessed with shoes.

## SHOPPING WEAKNESS

### GEMMA'S SHOES:

I bought these Alexander McQueen shoes from Harvey Nichols in Manchester but I had them in the garage for ages because I moved house. I've only just found them again and I love them.

### HOLLIE'S SCARVES:

My weakness is Alexander McQueen scarves – I have seventeen of them, and two skull rings.

### JENNIFER'S DRESSES:

Dresses are my shopping weakness. The D&G leopard-print one is my favourite of all three – it's gorgeous. The black one is Roberto Cavalli. I've only worn it once, to the NTA awards, but it's a classic. The white one is by Camilla and Marc. I wore to the Inside Soap Awards and it seemed like a good idea at the time though looking back I think it made me a bit too booby.

**“ Mixing designer with high street is always good. I wore a black Hervé Léger skirt to the TRIC awards once and teamed it with a dress from Wallis that I customized into a top ”** *Jennifer*

**“ I've got red shoes on and my hair in a pony tail and I think my belly looks like a potbelly ”** *Jorgie*

*Opposite — Top left:* Claire at the National TV Awards 2007 / *Centre:* Gemma won Best Comedy Performance at the 2007 British Soap Awards / *Top right:* Jennifer in a Hervé Léger dress at the British Soap Awards in 2008 / *Bottom left:* Hollie-Jay at the British Soap Awards 2009 / *Bottom right:* Jorgie at the British Soap Awards 2009

friends & family

chapter 4

With all that bitching and hair pulling onscreen – it's easy (and secretly a bit fun) to imagine that the fireworks spill across into the real lives of the stars too. So, what do they really think of each other behind the scenes? Have they ever fallen out? Who do they turn to for advice? Who's best mates with who? And who's the most neurotic? We're about to find out. Jen, Claire, Gemma, Hollie and Jorgie also open up about their very different backgrounds and reveal who it was that shaped who they are today. As the girls remember their childhood, we discover they got told off for just the same things as we did (coming home drunk for the first time and throwing parties behind your parents' backs, anyone?) and they talk honestly about everything from the awkwardness of buying their first bra to the trauma of losing a parent or being abandoned by your dad . . .

# Don't tell me what to do!

**" My mum drove past me and I had a bottle of booze in my hand. She got out the car and told me off. It was so embarrassing! "**

*Jorgie Porter*

---

### Were you well behaved as a kid?

**JEN** I was quite good – my mum worries about me more now than she did back then! I was only grounded a few times for stupid things like painting on the back of my house or setting some twigs on fire. I was a bit of a tomboy and would hang around with loads of lads.

**GEMMA** I was a proper tomboy too. My mum would dress me in beautiful things and do my hair all nicely and I'd come home with everything ripped and hanging off me. I was obsessed with Popeye. I used to do this face like Popeye does – so in all these family pictures I've got my mouth half opened and a squinty look on my face like he had. They thought I had a twitch or something. It was very unattractive. Oh, and I used to hold my breath when I had a tantrum. That can't have been pleasant for my parents!

**HOLLIE** My mum always used to laugh at me. I was a little diva and would tell people what to do! Saying that, though, I wasn't really naughty because I was working from the age of 15 in *Grange Hill*.

**CLAIRE** I was quite feisty and, let's say, challenging as a teenager. I argued about anything and everything – my brother getting in my way, people chewing their food too loud – the lot. My brother was really quiet and gentle and Mum said I was like a creature from another planet when I arrived. I didn't speak English until I was four.

## What do you mean?!

**CLAIRE** I spoke in a made-up language! I would refuse to speak English. It was like gobbledegook but sort of made sense because I had my own words for different things. My mum tried to speak it back to me and my brother even learnt it too! They took me to the doctor's and did some tests because they thought I was deaf or had some sort of learning problem. But the doctor said, 'No, she's just choosing to do this deliberately.' Eventually I snapped out of it.

## Do you still speak in it now?

**CLAIRE** I sleep talk now, and Mum is convinced that sometimes it's that same mumbo-jumbo.

## What's your relationship like with your family?

**GEMMA** I've got a brother and sister who are a lot older than me, which means I'm very close to my mum and dad, because it was the three of us mostly. I was like an only child. My mum and dad are amazing – I always make time for them. My fiancé Ian and I cook a roast for them every Sunday.

**HOLLIE** I've got a huge family. I've got two brothers; I live with my younger brother and my mum and my stepdad – I recently moved back home to Manchester, which I love because it means getting looked after! And my older brother lives in the house we bought together. He's about to have a baby with his missus. Then my dad has two daughters, who have also then got another sister. There are loads! The McQueens might seem crazy to some people but to me they seem quite normal. I have something like 24 cousins – and most of us are girls. Our family weddings make the McQueens look tame!

**CLAIRE** I've got quite a small family – an older brother, my mum and dad. We're close though.

**JORGIE** I've always lived with my grandma; she's been my second mum. Her and my mum brought me up together because I've never known my dad. He left when I was born. I've never known anything different so I'm pretty happy. And I'm really chuffed that my grandma's still around. [Smiles] And Mum knows everything – she's like my best friend. I was free to do a lot and play out till late – if Mum wouldn't let me do something I'd go and ask Grandma instead!

## Can you talk about the absence of your dad?

**JORGIE** I don't remember him ever being in my life. I was born and he left and didn't want to have anything to do with me, or so it seemed. [Shrugs] I've never known any different. People think they're offending me when they mention their dads or say that it's Father's Day, but it's cool. It's just the way it is for me. And to be honest, I feel so much love from being brought up by my mum and grandma.

## How does it affect you when you think about him?

**JORGIE** It does affect me a bit, I suppose, because he knows about me and if he'd wanted to meet me he would have done so by now. He has another daughter, too; he had her after me, and she actually went to my primary school. I remember the day I found out. It was after gymnastics one night and my mum was sitting with me in the car looking all serious – my dad was coming down the road. It was the first time I'd laid eyes on him. He was with my sister and I remember him chatting to my mum a bit but he didn't say much to me. And that was it. I've never known why he left or what happened. I don't get emotional about it, though. I feel like I'm better for how I was brought up. You know what he looked like? A penguin. [Laughs] You know those funny ones with the blond whiskers by their eyes?

## Do you ever think about meeting up with your sister?

**JORGIE** We've got some mutual friends on Facebook and I have thought about it, but when I get to know her I want to be a proper big sister. I want to be able to drive and pick her up and look after her. I just don't feel it's the right time yet. Also, it's hard to spend time with someone when you don't know them. I find it hard enough making time for my real friends as it is.

## What do you think about your dad now?

**JORGIE** I sometimes wonder whether he has a personality like mine; it might make me understand myself a bit more. I'm more laid-back than my mum so I wonder if that has anything to do with him. No, I've honestly never shed a tear about him. I don't know. Maybe I've buried some feelings, I don't go that deep about it. [Shrugs]

**HOLLIE** I used to play my mum and dad off against each other! I used to get money off my mum and then tell my dad I didn't have any. I was so cheeky.

**JEN** My dad passed away when I was a teenager so my mum is like my best mate. My auntie Joan is like an Irish nutcase! One of my brothers is just like me and the other's a bit quieter.

## What was it like for you when your dad passed away?

**JEN** Horrible. But I was just numb. He had bowel cancer and I remember finding out when I was 14 – I'd just come back from holiday with my friend. I was in the car with my mum and I didn't know what to ask her, I didn't understand it properly. She told me it was a tumour and I said, 'Oh, so that means it's not cancer?' I was in denial and I just felt a bit blank. She was certain he'd get better and so was I – he was my dad, I thought he was invincible. He had to go for loads of treatment. I helped him every step of the way. I would do anything at all for him. Even though he had radiotherapy he still looked so well. He didn't lose his hair or his athletic build and his skin was really glowing. That's why I couldn't believe it was serious. But then I remember him looking at me and saying, 'They can't do anything for me, love.'

## When did you know he was going to die?

**JEN** He went into Manor Lands Home and that's when Mum told me it was terminal. I still don't think it sunk in, though – even when Mum told me, 'It's going to be tonight.' I remember having to go and get some stuff so I could stay the night and see him for the last time and I was crying because I didn't want to see him die. There was a room where you could play on the PlayStation next door to where he was and I met my cousin James there and played with him most of the time while my mum sat with my dad. Now I look back on it I think: you stupid little girl, you wasted all that time you could have spent with him. But kids deal with stuff in their own way. It was just how I did it. I don't know what went through my head. I remember I did go in and speak to him for a long time before he died. I spent days after his death helping to plan his funeral, making cards and writing a poem. But in the end I was too overwhelmed to read it out at the service. I began but the words wouldn't come out, and as I started crying the priest had to take over. I insisted on playing Puff Daddy's 'I'll Be Missing You', and putting a cuddly cat called Felix in his coffin so he wouldn't be by himself and would have some company. It was weird how I dealt with it after that. It was a bit of a blur.

## How did it affect you later on?

**JEN** He had this tatty old cardigan that he always wore and after he'd died I slept in it every night for three years. Now I snuggle into it whenever I'm missing him. Mum and I talk about him all the time and there are loads of moments when I think of stuff I'd like to tell him, things that remind me what a Dad-sized hole there is left in my life. But ultimately his death taught me that if I could cope with losing him when I was only 15, then I could cope with anything. I've also learnt that I've got to get a new buzz out of every day because you never know what life has in store.

## Is that what brought you so close to your mum?

**JEN** I think so. I tell her everything now. Before that I would always talk to my dad about girlie stuff – even when I started my period! Although he thought I said I'd just farted instead of that I'd just started! [Laughs]

**GEMMA** I started my period when I was 13 and when it happened my mum took me to dance classes as usual and proceeded to tell everyone. She said to me, 'This means you're older now and you can have babies.' Babies! At 13!

**CLAIRE** I was going through a real temper stage when I was about 13 so I think my mum presumed I was starting my period, even when I wasn't. She sat me on the stairs and gave me these sanitary pads and explained what was going to happen, then packed me off to school. But because I was a gymnast it held off and I didn't get my period until years later. I was nearly 16 when it happened.

**JEN** Two days after I started I had a baton-twirling competition – I was in the majorettes. My mum gave me a tampon and I said, 'I can't put it up there!' I got it halfway in and it hurt so much that I thought it's not going up any more. I was in agony. So instead I put on a sanitary towel, two pairs of knickers, two of those 'pull you in' knickers and two pairs of shimmery tights. I couldn't move! But the worst thing was that when I got there my mum had told my mate's mum, who turned out to have a big gob! [Laughs]

**CLAIRE** I didn't like the idea of a tampon at all.

**HOLLIE** Me neither – I was so scared about it hurting. I didn't know what on earth to do.

## What about your first bra?

**JEN** I loved it! My mum got me an AA from Asda. I think I went out with socks down my bra at one stage for added effect. After that

I sprouted quite quickly and soon got my first Wonderbra, a black one, which I thought was amazing.

**GEMMA** I watched *Home and Away* when Sally got her first bra and I wanted one but I didn't have any boobs at that age. So I went to Tammy Girl with my mum and nana to get one so I looked like Sally.

**HOLLIE** I think I bought my own! I got it from Tammy Girl too.

**CLAIRE** I remember Tammy Girl!

**HOLLIE** I bought all these thongs too and thought I was really cool – they said things like 'Heartbreaker' and 'I'm a moose'.

**CLAIRE** The first bra we all wore used to be those little crop tops that fastened at the back and I was so excited when Mum said I could have one. I didn't have boobs for years. Although I can't really claim to have amazing assets now! The only time I experienced bigger boobs was when I went on a certain pill – and they grew to a C cup. Shame I was an absolute lunatic and had to stop taking it. [Laughs]

## Do you remember coming home drunk for the first time?

**JEN** My auntie Joan used to run this football team called the Bradford Allstars and I was about 14 and I snuck in a couple of pints when I was out with her. I got home and my mum said, 'Are you alright?' Two minutes later I was throwing up all over the place. She wasn't happy with my auntie Joan!

**JORGIE** I remember being caught! I was walking along with my mates and had a massive bottle in my hand and my mum was driving round the roundabout and she saw me, got out of the car and stopped me. She was like, 'Jorge, what the hell are you doing?'

**GEMMA** My mum and dad didn't see me drunk until Jen came to my house after we'd started on *Hollyoaks*. She was the one who let it out of the bag! I had been so careful until then.

**CLAIRE** I concealed it pretty well – I'd leg it upstairs before mum could notice.

**HOLLIE** I threw a house party and thought I'd got away with it – my mum had only gone to the pub. I don't know what I was thinking! I wanted to be cool. But I honestly thought we'd covered our tracks. The thing that gave it away was peppercorns in the fish tank and vinegar all over the fruit. I was grounded for two months.

## Did you keep a diary?

**CLAIRE** I got one every year but never had anything to write in it!

**JEN** I used to keep one when I was younger – I'd write about Prince William and Peter Andre – I loved them!

**GEMMA** I hope your opinion has changed since then!

**JEN** I still think Prince William's pretty hot, but Harry's a bit sexier – he seems more naughty. Peter Andre looks a bit too groomed now for my liking. I like my men a bit rougher.

**CLAIRE** I was having a really stressy day recently and went to Nicole [who plays Myra McQueen] for advice. She told me I should keep a diary so I could write down my thoughts and feelings. But I don't want it there on paper – it's all up here in my head and that's bad enough. [Laughs]

## How have your parents influenced you?

**JEN** Massively. When I'm a parent I just want to do it how they did. They gave me freedom to make my own choices but in doing so I felt so much respect and loyalty to them that I was always well behaved. I was allowed to do so much more than my mates were but I felt trusted. And I think that's the best thing you can do. I've had friends whose parents were really strict with them and they've gone right off the rails. It's probably a scary thing to do – give your child all that freedom – but I always felt loved at the same time, so I would never do anything that would disrespect them.

**GEMMA** My mum and dad gave me freedom, which is a good thing because it means you never want to let them down. The only thing they were strict about was having boyfriends – I wasn't allowed one until I was 17. I couldn't top how my mum and dad have been as parents but I'm in no hurry to have kids. When I was a kid I used to have about 30 dolls because I loved babies. That can wait now, though! My dogs are like my babies anyway.

**HOLLIE** My mum has taught me to think twice about choosing names for my kids!

## Why?!

**HOLLIE** She's a bit of a Michael Jackson fan and when I was born she nearly called me Billie-Jean Bowes. But luckily my dad protested and pointed out that I would get such stick for it at school if I was 'Billie Bowes'! I think I still had it for a couple of days before she relented.

**JORGIE** If I could be half the parent my mum is I'd be happy. She's dead outgoing, extremely funny and gets on with everyone. When we walk around near where we live she gets stopped by people left right and centre! They all want to talk to her all the time.

# Friends and foes

## " Me, Gemma and Claire have alter egos who send each other text messages "

*Jennifer Metcalfe*

**Are you still in touch with your mates from home?**

**JEN** Yes totally. I make sure I go back to Leeds to see them as much as possible. The Jen I am with them is who I consider to be the real, proper me. They make me feel so at ease. Sometimes, being in this industry, it's easy to get wrapped up in how you look and what's expected of you. But with my friends at home I can sit and just laugh for hours – it's amazing.

**JORGIE** I am! I've known my best friend from college and literally can't live without speaking to her for a day. She's called Sophia Chan – she's Chinese – but we all call her Chan. There's also Mary and Marie who I'm dead close to since my school days.

**How do you keep in touch?**

**JEN** We BlackBerry-message each other about 50 times a day!

**CLAIRE** I have an amazing network of friends and there's one – my best friend Amy – who I'm really close to. They're an important part of my life – and what's nice is that they know my friends from the show now. Jen, Gemma and I often go out together and invite our other mates.

## What kind of mate are you?

**GEMMA** I'm a good listener, I'm always there for my friends whenever they need me. I'm also very loyal.

**JEN** A very good listener. Fun, loyal and trustworthy.

**CLAIRE** I'm a really solid friend. I've still got all my mates from school so I'd like to think that 15 years of being friends with someone means I've been quite good to them. I've got some great friends on *Hollyoaks* too. I give as much as they give me – sometimes a little bit more. [Grins]

**HOLLIE** I'm the sort of friend who gets on with everyone and tries to make everyone laugh. I'm a good listener and sometimes I give good advice – but I can never sort out my own problems!

## Who are your best friends on set?

**JEN** Gemma and Claire. Claire's pretty straight up with you – so if you're emotionally unstable, forget it. [Laughs] If you need some sympathy, don't go there!

**CLAIRE** It's true!

**JEN** Sometimes when I'm having boy problems I want to be able to go on and on about it all day and I want someone to listen. Claire's not really interested but that's good in a way, because it makes me get a grip. Gemma's very sympathetic; she's good for cuddles and makes you feel really cared for.

**HOLLIE** Mine are Jorgie Porter and Kieron Richardson [plays Ste Hay]. Even though Kieron and me don't work together we have a history because we started at the same time, we grew up on the show together. We moved to the same apartment block together a while ago and bought our dogs at the same time! We hang out as much as possible. We're really close – but we don't need to be in regular contact to know each other's there. That's a rarity. It's a really beautiful friendship because there's no insecurity there. And Jorgie and me give each other so much advice, don't we?

**JORGIE** We try to!

**HOLLIE** We're bad with it though – we're so dramatic about our boy troubles. She's like a motivator who always tries to make me speak to boys. We actually only really got to know each other during the *Hollyoaks Later* shows. She's brilliant.

**JORGIE** Aaah, thanks! Yes, I'm close to Hollie-Jay and Saira Choudhry [plays Anita Roy]. If I ever fell out with Saira I'd do everything I could to make it right again with her. She's amazing. Hollie's especially good with my man troubles. So is Claire, because I lived with her for a while so she's good with advice on stuff like that and knows me well. If I've got a problem at work, Gemma's sorted me out before; she's stuck up for me and said, 'This isn't fair.'

## Who do you go to for advice?

**CLAIRE** It depends on the problem. Out of my mates on the set of *Hollyoaks*, I will go to Jen for everything – be it men, body problems or not feeling well. Leah who played Tina in the show is great too and we're still all really close. And Nicole, who plays my mum, Myra McQueen. Jen's advice is never biased; she's not one of those people who will just try to make you feel better, she'll tell me straight but in a kind way. That's the sort of advice I need.

**GEMMA** I'll turn to Jen and Leah for most things. Jen's good when you've had a boozy night and feel really guilty or embarrassed the next day. Leah's very good if you have any life worries; if you're having boy trouble she's good. Nicole's great too – she'll see everyone's point of view. [Pauses] But sometimes you just want to be pissed off and don't want to see any other point of view!

## Describe your relationship with the other girls on set.

**CLAIRE** Jenny, Gemma and I are especially close – we are genuinely like sisters. We annoy each other and we love each other, but after three years we've never had any raging rows – touch wood! There are moments when we disagree but it blows over by the next day. I lived with Jorgie for a while and had a lot of fun with her – we just had the giggles all the time, she's so sweet. I'm not as close to Hollie because she lives in Manchester so has to travel back there every night. But we did go to Spain together for a long weekend once, which was nice – and we have the same taste in music.

**JORGIE** I love Hollie-Jay when she's outside of work – she's such a different person, she's really funny. Claire is a bit wise and stuff but she's surprisingly hilarious. Gemma's nice to talk to about life things, and she's good at advice about womanly, grown-up stuff. Jen is mad and I can relate to her a lot because she's grown up like me, from a good family who's not necessarily rich but has a good grounding.

**JEN** Me and Claire spend so much time together at the moment that we speak each other's thoughts. I would say we're pretty close!

**CLAIRE** We keep sending pictures to each other too. We've got alter egos that we've created.

**JEN** When we're bored or one of us is a bit down we send them.

**CLAIRE** I'm 'Bernadette McCauley', who's like some fussy and finicky old woman who likes squirrels and falls over all the time.

**JEN** And I'm 'Ruby Malone', who just goes crazy all the time and pulls weird faces. Gemma's 'Maisy McDrake', who's off her head and likes loads of sex. One of my exes joined in at one point and he was called 'Rufus Wrong'un'. [All laugh]

**CLAIRE** So there were all these pictures of us in weird positions or doing stupid faces flying between mobiles! It's basically making yourself look as horrible as you can.

## How did it start?

**CLAIRE** I just sent a picture of myself to her one day and said, 'This is Bernadette McCauley – who are you?' I didn't even need to tell her what I was doing – she just did it!

**JEN** I send her things like, 'This is what your face would look like if it was a sperm'!

**CLAIRE** I took a series of pictures of Bernadette when I had an allergy attack once.

**JEN** Claire's always got allergies.

**CLAIRE** I had tissues all round me – the trick is to move when you're taking the picture too so you look a bit long-faced and blurry.

## What are you all like when you go out?

**JEN** Me and Gemma used to go out all the time – but she's recently settled down with her fiancé Ian. If I ever ask her to go out she's still well up for it though – we're very good on a night out together, we both have a drink and a big dance. Claire's a bit crackers, I love her to death. She'll do random things when we're out like get someone to start clapping at me. We'll tend to go out for meals quite a bit too – and she's got to know my mates from Leeds so we sometimes all go out together. Loads of my friends text Claire so it's nice to be able to combine it.

# Wise words

**" Claire always sends us quotes to inspire us each day – but we just laugh at them most of the time! "**

*Gemma Merna*

## Have you had any mentors in your life?

**CLAIRE** I think they've come in and out of my life in different stages – whether it's a producer of *Hollyoaks* or a great friend. On every job I've done I've learnt something from someone – I did a national tour of a play and there was an old-school actress working with us; she was 80 years old and so glamorous. I learnt so much from her about the etiquette of theatre, which was charming. I think my friends are mentors too – they all have an effect on me and how I am. And my mum is obviously a big influence on me – she will always give me advice and support me.

**JEN** For me it's definitely my friends. If you have a problem they'll tell you the truth. There are certain things that happen to you – especially where boys are concerned – and while you might forget them, your friends always remember the heartache. They're there to tell you in no uncertain terms not to go there again. It might upset you and you might fall out over it, but it's important.

**GEMMA** My mentor is a man called Mark Hudson who's the drama coach at *Hollyoaks*. When I first met him I was so scared of him because he had such a presence. I had to sing in front of him when I was 16 – but he got me through my nerves and gave me a lead role. He's known me for so long and so well and he made me realize I was more talented than I gave myself credit for. That's why I'm where I am today – he gave me the confidence I was lacking.

**CLAIRE** I do think people come in and out of your life, not like guardian angels but almost like mentors to get you through different stages. Like soul mates. Some stick with you and others will get you through certain parts and move on.

## Are there any mottos you live by?

**HOLLIE** Everything happens for a reason. Or shit happens!

**CLAIRE** I have loads! I use them on my BlackBerry Messenger and I put a different quote up on there each day for everyone to read.

**JEN** She writes them every day and it makes me laugh!

**GEMMA** Claire with her daily quotes! They're hilarious. I have to skim through them – I don't really take them in if I'm honest! I'm not really a quote person. To me what's going to happen happens. I believe in fate. Be yourself and believe in yourself: that's it.

**JORGIE** My motto is live for today. I could never think of a different quote every day though – I'm not that deep!

**CLAIRE** I put a quote up the other day about your life being a big sum of all the choices you make, which is so true. I find a different quote for every single day and it's interesting because they touch people in different ways. There's a website called *ThinkExist* that helps you find something relevant to the mood you're in that day.

**JEN** [Laughs] I read them and think: she's being all weird again!

**CLAIRE** Sometimes I might do a quote from a song though and I know Jen'll like them. I nearly did a Missy Elliott one the other day that said 'Sex me so good I say blah-blah-blah'.

**JEN** That would have been a good one!

**CLAIRE** But I didn't do it because I thought, well, that's a lie because no one's sexing me so good! [Laughs]

**JEN** My motto is float like a butterfly, sting like a big fat-arsed bee! [Laughs]

## What about any 'inspirational' books?

**GEMMA** I read a few self-help books when I was 17 or 18 and didn't know where I was going in my life. [Laughs] But now I'm more about believing if you're nice to people then you'll be rewarded. I feel I'm at a nice stage in my life and just trust myself at the moment.

**CLAIRE** I've read loads! I love *Life of Pi*, which is about philosophy; I think everybody should read that. *1984* by George Orwell is incredible too. There are some really cool plays that have inspired me too – one called *Seascape with Sharks and Dancer* – by Don Nigro. Another called *Extremities*.

**JEN** Claire told me to read *The Secret*, which I've nearly finished.

**CLAIRE** You should listen to it on audio really and go to bed with it.

**JEN** But I'd have it mixed up with all my songs and then one of them would wake me up blaring in my ear!

**CLAIRE** To be honest, I'd fall asleep listening to *Secret* and then I'd suddenly wake up thinking: who's that? [Laughs]

**JEN** I can't sleep with anything in my ear; it has to be pitch black and deadly silent.

**HOLLIE-JAY**

**JORGIE'S** so much fun and really cheeky. Whenever there's a lull on set she'll start dancing. At every available opportunity.

**JEN** is either trumping or on her BlackBerry 24/7!

**CLAIRE** is eccentric, funny and unexpected. And she sleep-talks all the time. She can move her eyes in opposite directions and is always doing funny voices.

**JEN** loves the same tunes as me, she loves dirty rap. And she has the dirtiest laugh of anyone I've ever met!

**HOLLIE** eats too much sushi. She needs to stop visiting sushi restaurants and play with me more!

**GEMMA** gives me cookies between scenes. I share a changing room with her and she feeds me M&S chocolate-chip ones. When I'm hungry she'll look after me.

**JORGIE**

**JEN**

**CLAIRE** is most likely to be found pulling a funny face in a corner on her own.

**HOLLIE'S** most likely to be texting someone.

**GEMMA** is most likely to be petting her dogs and baking a cake.

**JORGIE'S** always smiling!

**CLAIRE'S** always messaging everyone with a little quote for the day and a picture of what she's wearing. It's like her own little fashion shoot and it makes me laugh.

**JEN** is my best friend. You're most likely to find her on the toilet – she's always there!

**JORGIE** makes me smile all the time, she's such a gorgeous person. Like a ray of sunshine. I don't think she's ever unhappy.

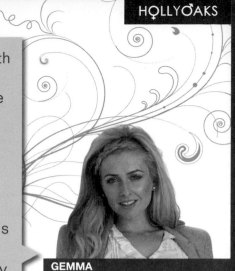

GEMMA

**JORGIE** is my little bosom buddy. She's like a human play centre. Always fun to be around.

**JEN'S** a rock to me. I couldn't imagine life without her. We're business partners, best friends and we're there for each other.

**GEMMA** is one of my best mates. She's building a house at the moment so you're most likely to find her running around with bricks, a spade and her dogs – she's an amazing friend and over the last year she's found a peace within herself and it's a really beautiful quality.

**HOLLIE'S** a little firework. She's a real character and can be misunderstood sometimes but she's got a warm heart. She just needs to realize that people love her for who she is.

CLAIRE

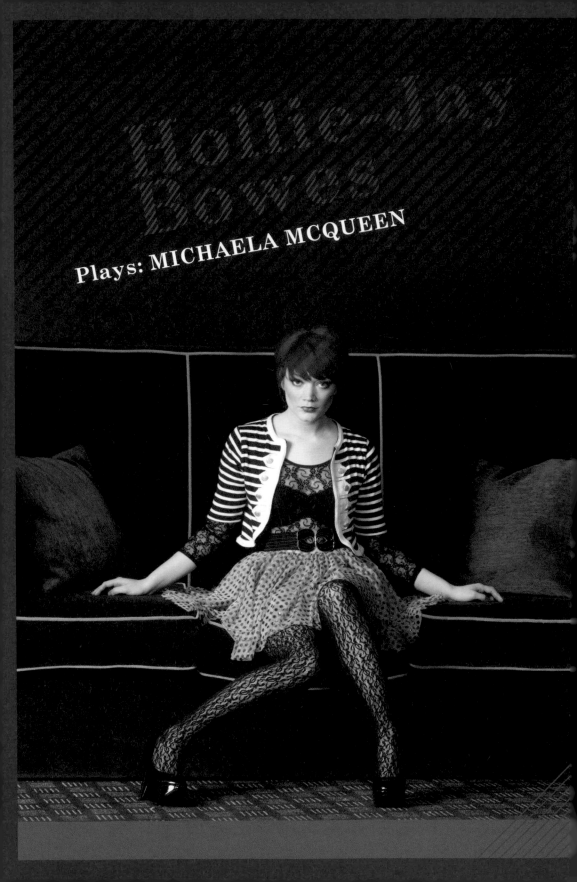

**Birthday:**
17.01.89. I'm a Capricorn.
I'm really sad in that I always
believe what the horoscopes
say. Capricorns are meant to
be creative and really good
with interiors apparently! I'm
quite creative, lose my head
quite quick and have a bit
of a defence barrier up.

**Most likely to send a text saying:**
'Mwaaaaaaah xxx love you' I
send that to all my friends or
my mum practically every day.

**Fave body part:**
The top half of my stomach
because that's the tiniest part
of me. I've got alright boobs
as well – they're little which
means they're quite pert.

**Dislike most about myself:**
My bum, I hate it. I'm pale, freckly
and I've got naturally red hair – so
going on holiday for me is really
awful. When I go on holiday the
one thing I hate is getting the
back of my legs and my bum out
– I've always got a sarong on until
I get into the actual pool and the
sarong's always waiting at the
side. I'd love nothing more than to

**Bet you didn't know that . . .**
I'm absolutely wicked at the
Cereal Box Game – which is when
you have a cereal box when you're
really drunk, you cut an inch off
every time and you've got to pick
it up with your teeth and you're
not allowed your knees, your
hands or your elbows to touch the
floor. I can pick it up off the floor
when it's about a centimetre!

have a skinny bum and a boyish
figure – but I guess you always
want what you haven't got.

**Last lie told:**
I told my mum I'd walked
the dog when I hadn't.

**Most embarrassing moment:**
The other girls won't be
bothered by this because they
love doing it. But my idea of
absolute hell in an embarrassing
situation is when I trump.

**Biggest fashion faux pas:**
When I'd first started on
*Hollyoaks* and I was about 16,
I wore cream lace tights, a
cream lace top, brown shoes, a
brown skirt and a brown jacket.

What's worse is that I was being interviewed on a TV show!

**My co-stars would describe me as:**
Funny and weird.

**Proudest moment:**
Buying a house with my brother when I was 18.

**Favourite flavour cheese:**
Cheese with cranberries in – that's well nice.

**Biggest regret:**
Wasting a lot of money on an ex-boyfriend.

**Most expensive thing I've ever bought (apart from car and house):**
A Chloe dress, which cost £980. I bought it for the British Soap Awards because I wanted to be really posh.

**Top three happy tunes:**
'Rock the Casbah' by The Clash, Imogen Heap's 'Headlock' and even though it's not very happy content, I like 'You Overdid It Doll' by the Courteeners.

**My friends call me . . .**
Hollie or Hollie-Jay. My name was originally Hollie-Jean but I changed it when I was 13 because at that age Jean really wasn't that cool. But my mates call me Jeanie sometimes.

**Last time I cried:**
Yesterday morning because I felt sick. I can't handle feeling sick – I'm a proper precious little girl, and I can't handle it.

**What makes me laugh:**
Really stupid random stuff. Me and my best friend Lucy have got this thing where I put my arm out and make a stupid sound. I don't know why but it makes us laugh – every time she feels a bit down she makes me do it.

**If I want to treat myself . . .**
I go to Topshop.

Hollie-Jay – Hollyoaks Calendar 2009

body talk

chapter 5

body 4

From the outside of *Hollyoaks* looking in, we see a plethora of perfect body shapes, girls with legs that go up to their armpits, tummies as taut as torpedoes and smiles that could melt ice-caps. But inside the make-up room, nestled at the back of the imaginary set of Chester in a suburban estate in Liverpool, it's a refreshingly different story. In this chapter we learn how the *Hollyoaks* actresses really see themselves in the mirror and how in some cases their preened exterior masks a heap of insecurities about the way they look. Below the surface they're just like us. They too have 'fat days' when they think their stomach has bloated to the size of a ship. The only difference is that they don't have the option of hiding behind their desk for the day – their day at work means squeezing into tight dresses and skimpy clothes (maybe not such fun after all!). Being in the spotlight can mean their body worries seem magnified. Here we scrape beneath the shiny, bronze-powdered surface to reveal how the *Hollyoaks* girls genuinely feel about their looks. They speak frankly about struggling with their weight, mad crazy diets, cellulite and crying in front of the mirror because they feel uglier than their co-stars . . .

# What I see in the mirror

## " Have I ever cried looking in the mirror? Loads of times! "

*Claire Cooper*

### How do you feel about your looks?

**JEN** I look at my face and body and say to myself, 'That's alright.' I'm very realistic about my body. But my body bloats and de-bloats like mad – one week I can look like I seriously need to put on some pounds and the next I look all ballooned. My lifestyle's all over the place so one week I might not be in work, I can go to the gym and eat healthily, and the next I might go to three parties in a row which will mean eating and drinking loads.

**GEMMA** I'm much more comfortable about myself now than when I was a teenager – I can actually bear to look in the mirror. [Laughs] When I was younger I used to focus on every small part of me so much that I'd always find something I hated. I think that's a big part of growing up in this country – people are so used to being dissatisfied – whereas we should just love things the way they're meant to be.

**CLAIRE** Despite saying that, we have to look at ourselves in the mirror on a daily basis so you're always going to see bad things! Working on a show like *Hollyoaks* means you do over-analyse yourself, more than you might in a different job. It's especially noticeable for me because I have to dress up as Jacqui McQueen! My hair's naturally curly but when I play Jacqui I have to have it scraped right back off my head. I think it's fair to say that I don't help myself looks-wise on the show. But at the same time I wouldn't have it any other way. Besides, my parents made me – it would be a bit of an insult if I told them I didn't like the way I looked!

**HOLLIE** When I look at myself in the mirror I just think of myself as a bit of a ginger monster! I haven't got over that complex from my school days. I dye my hair – have done since I was in my teens – it's probably been every other colour under the sun than its natural ginger hue since then. I also think my features are a bit weird. I remember being in the live audience at *Dancing on Ice* watching my co-star Kieron Richardson when he was in the show and the cameras pointed at me so that my face came up on the giant TV screen in the stadium, and I just thought: I have got the oddest face! I [Shrugs]

**JORGIE** One of the things I always notice when I look in the mirror is that my eyes change colour: sometimes they're green and sometimes they're blue! At the moment I'm feeling quite good about myself – I think I'm about the right size for my frame and my skin's much better than it has been in the past. When I was at college I used to be quite a bit bigger and really spotty with a brace on my teeth. My hair used to break off too because I bleached it so often. The strange thing is that, even then, I was a bit oblivious to the mirror and thought I looked OK. Well, until people shouted, 'Oi, pizza face!'

**JEN** I suffered from acne up until only about two years ago. I had to go to the doctor's all the time because it wasn't calming down – and when I saw myself on camera after starting *Hollyoaks* all I could focus on when I watched the scene back were lumps everywhere, it was horrible. Luckily the doctor changed my pill and gave me antibiotics so it's cleared up now. But like Claire said, working on a

TV show means you can't hide what you look like if you're having a bad day. On *Hollyoaks* you're 'on display' all the time.

**JORGIE** [Smiles] When I spend a lot of time with people I stare at them so often that I think I look like them and then get a shock when I go to the mirror. Does that make sense?

**CLAIRE** You're a mentalist!

**JORGIE** I just get a shock sometimes because I don't realize what I look like. It might be because I think personality is more important than looks so I just don't think of them that much. You can always put make-up on and stuff to make you look a bit better anyway.

## Have you ever cried when you've looked in the mirror?

**CLAIRE** Yeah! Loads. I've had plenty of feeling-sorry-for-myself moments. [Laughs]. Once when I was at school I had eczema all over my face and couldn't get rid of it – I looked like a panda.

**GEMMA** I do. I cry all the time! My dad used to turn round to me and say, 'There can be no more tears left in you, Gemma!' I'm just very dramatic – now poor Ian has to put up with it.

**CLAIRE** The thing with me is that I will cry and put all my emotions on someone if I'm in a relationship, but if I'm single I hold it in and get quite hardened.

**JORGIE** I've cried many times too – over my hair being too short, having a brace – all sorts.

**HOLLIE** When people talk about the *Hollyoaks* girls being gorgeous – I see that, but I've always thought: that's not me. But I do also have days when I look in the mirror and I look nice; sometimes it's even when I've got no make-up on first thing in the morning or when I've still got make-up on from the night before and it's smudged in all the right places.

# Body battles

## " I was always aspiring to be something else "

*Gemma Merna*

---

**How much bigger were you when you were younger?**

---

**GEMMA** I went to dance school and I had big womanly hips from the age of 13. All I remember thinking was: no one else looks like me. When I was very young I was really chunky and I think that's what's made me worry as I've got older. Also, coming from a dancing and theatre background affects you more because everyone is so, so thin. I'd look at the older girls and none of them would be eating, while I'd be sat there with my crisps and a chocolate bar from the packed lunch my mum made me. [Laughs]

**CLAIRE** I was a gymnast for ten years so I've always been slim. I eat what I want but not huge quantities – and that's how I've always been. My weight doesn't really change.

**HOLLIE** I'm probably the smallest now that I've ever been. I used to feel like a big ginger freak every time I looked in the mirror.

**JORGIE** I was at dance college too and just like Gemma's experience, my size was noticeable because the rest of the dancers were so skinny. I think also I was bigger back then because I was on the pill – which meant that I ballooned a bit in weight – I hadn't found one that suited me properly. Plus, I went out drinking a bit too much.

## What did you think of your looks back then?

**JORGIE** I thought: there will come a time when I decide I'm going to sort myself out, I'll be skinny one day, but one day didn't come for three years. I just held it off because I was still happy in myself.

**GEMMA** I was the sort of person who would look through magazines and want to look like Barbie. I thought that was perfection. It's weird how your mind works when you're younger. I was always aspiring to be something else. I didn't used to like wearing bikinis at all as I got older either. But I've realized you can't change your body type.

**CLAIRE** Aside from having eczema when I was younger, I had operations on my eye so it was bloodshot for years. I was squint.

**GEMMA** How unfortunate!

**CLAIRE** [Laughs] I know! My first operation was when I was 5, then I had another operation at 11 and the surgery went a bit wrong so I had to have another one when I was 18. But because of that, when I looked at myself, it was my eye I noticed, nothing about my body. My parents were always very positive about life and accepting who you are, though, and I think that made a difference.

## What were the bits you liked the least?

**GEMMA** I was shocking when I was younger – I gave myself such a hard time. Fat bum, fat legs, fat belly, fat arms, everything – it was ridiculous. It really affected me loads – I wouldn't try on certain clothes because I didn't think they suited me. I just was never happy.

**CLAIRE** I was the opposite. I've never had a major complex about how I looked. My friends were all very similar so there was nothing to compare. Although because I did gymnastics my body took a bit longer to develop than the other girls.

**JEN** My bum just seemed huge! It's always been that way – I've got quite a small frame so it looks even bigger than it is and even now when I put on a bit of weight you can really tell in that area. But I think back then a lot of it was puppy fat. [Pauses and laughs] Saying that, I did also used to chow down a lot! My diet was terrible.

## How have you changed over the years?

**HOLLIE** I think I've got more experimental – mainly with my hair. I'm going to go back to my natural colour of ginger again soon but my hair's too short at the moment – it needs to be longer to carry it off. I used to hate being a redhead but now I look at people with long red hair and think it's amazing – it's really weird. Florence and the Machine has helped change that for the gingers around the world. Although, that said, I don't want to do it while it's in fashion.

**GEMMA** I think as I've got older and accepted myself, the things I didn't like I've corrected. And if I get a bit of extra cellulite at Christmas or something I just think: I'll sort it out when it gets to summer! [Laughs]

**JEN** I remember the first time being aware of my body was when I was about 13 or 14 and I'd gone to this place called Clothing World with my mum, which was a clothes shop near our house in Bradford, and they had mirrors all the way round in the changing room. I looked at myself from the side and then from behind and I remember thinking: is that really me? Honestly, my bum was huge. I was in tears. I noticed my boobs had been growing too. Then I looked at my face from the side and it was like seeing someone for the first time, and I thought: my nose looks all pointy. I was in a right state that day! [Laughs] It was after that I started going to the gym and being conscious of how I looked. Because I didn't like what I saw.

# Food for thought

## " I tried the cabbage soup diet but it made me pump all the time! "

*Jorgie Porter*

---

### Did you watch what you ate when you were younger?

**JEN** No! My mum used to get this Cadbury's chocolate cake and I had about a third of it for breakfast every day plus about three or four biscuits, then it was off to the tuck shop at about 11 a.m. There I'd buy two Toffee Crisps, two packets of pickled onion Monster Munch and a Wham bar. At lunch time – and this is no word of a lie – I'd have chicken pie and chips every day and if they didn't have it in the canteen I'd be so upset! And I had a McDonald's three nights a week for my tea. [Pauses] If I hadn't stopped I'd be in trouble now.

**CLAIRE** I wasn't really allowed any of the bad stuff – Mum would always cook us casseroles. There might have been the odd night for fish fingers and chips though. And I remember sometimes coming home from school when my mum wasn't there and I'd get loads of vanilla ice cream out of the freezer and cover it with hundreds and thousands and scoff the lot!

**HOLLIE** It was all about chocolate for me. When I was really little I went through a phase of eating three bars of chocolate a day! I was only about six or seven and my mum kept trying to wean me off it and I remember saying, 'I'll try and cut down to one a day,' as if that was a real hardship! My mum said, 'That will be about seven bars a week!' I replied, 'But that's nothing, Mum – it could've been 35!' I still crave it now. Penguins are my favourite. Once I ran downstairs and tried to smuggle them in my knickers – I ran upstairs and they all fell out. Surprisingly.

**GEMMA** My mum fed me turkey burgers and chips, chicken drumsticks and chips – the lot! Back then I don't think there was so much of an obvious issue or focus on what you ate as a kid so it didn't seem a problem. I don't think I even knew what fruit was until I was about eight or nine. There was no Jamie Oliver telling us what to do then!

### Do you notice how eating and drinking affects your body?

**JEN** Definitely. Also because when I drink a lot I can't be bothered going to the gym. I always think that exercise comes second to anything else – if it was a choice between that and seeing my friends I would choose the latter any day.

**CLAIRE** With me I notice the effect of alcohol more in my face. My eyes feel like slit eyes, and my face shrinks so it's all tight! I go a funny colour too.

**JORGIE** Drinking definitely – it makes me blow up. And it makes me eat loads too. It's dangerous working in *Hollyoaks* too because the food in the canteen is so yummy. The English breakfasts are amazing and for a while I was having those every day but I had to stop.

**HOLLIE** I love going out on a Friday and getting drunk. I would never ever go out on a school night but the weekends are for partying. And I don't feel bloated afterwards! I know, I'm strange. Also I crave really healthy food when I'm hung-over whereas other people crave burgers. I do watch what drinks I have, though – I never have anything like liqueurs, which I think are really fattening.

**GEMMA** I'm quite in tune with my body – I know, when I've had a few to drink, how long it's going to take to come out of my system and make me feel normal again. Last time I had a drink it took me two weeks to get over it. I don't drink often so it really affects me.

## Some people are obsessive about dieting though . . .

**JEN** Yes and at times I have been guilty of that. But now, as long as I'm not overweight or really underweight then I just plod along and don't let it bother me. I had a time near last Christmas when I did feel really down about myself. I felt much bigger than usual and kept wearing really baggy clothes like extra large men's hoodies. The only option was to sort it out – go to the gym every day, eat healthily, and after a week I was back on track again. Then last week I felt dead skinny and today I feel fat again! [Laughs] You can't win with me!

## Have you tried any fad diets?

**JEN** I tried the Atkins diet for about a day when the big craze first came out – all these girls seemed to be losing nearly half a stone in a week and I just had to give it a go. The first morning I got up and thought: this is amazing, I'm allowed to eat all this bad stuff like cheese and bacon and eggs! I loved it. By the time night came I felt a bit sick, and by the next morning I had this craving for carbs. Too much protein makes you feel nauseous.

**HOLLIE** I did a diet that I made up myself which was chicken and celery soup for a week. Not ideal to do it constantly but I sometimes do it now for a couple of days if I want to detox.

**JORGIE** I did the cabbage soup diet for a week because the teachers at my dance college suggested I detox and lose a bit of weight if I wanted to be the top ballerina. But this diet gave me major pumps – I was letting them out all the time! I did lose weight but as soon as I came off it and started eating normally again I put it back on. I used to get a bit emotional with food though – whenever I was feeling a bit fat it would just make me go home and eat more.

**GEMMA** I've tried all sorts, like the 'no carbs after six', and I did the Gillian McKeith diet for a bit but that was hardly eating anything and I lost so much weight that my dad got worried about me. With some of those diets you need so much time to prepare the food it makes it virtually impossible to have a normal life – I was getting up at 6 a.m. to make soups for work, which was too much effort in the end. You need to have a life! I've learnt that you just need to eat a healthy and well-balanced diet most of the time – it's not rocket science.

**JEN** I just look at calories of things now – that's how I learnt how to manage my eating. I still have binges every now and again, though – whenever I'm hung-over I can sit and eat my body weight in chocolate three times over or gobble up bags of those Haribo sour sweets! It's hard when you're in restaurants too because even if I opt for the healthy choice I'm always tempted by desserts. So I need to stay away!

**HOLLIE** I know I need to cut down on carbs. I used to try and just eat protein but that would be wrong. I'm like Jen in that I calorie count now and know exactly how many I have in my body each day. But during the weekend I let myself have treats – that's when I can eat crap. I had a Chinese at midnight the other Saturday. Then Monday came and that was it, back to calorie counting.

# Working it out

## " I exercise to songs that sing about big butts because I've got one! "

*Jennifer Metcalfe*

---

### What sort of exercise do you do?

**HOLLIE** I walk on the treadmill for about 20 minutes – I don't run because it can make your legs bigger. Then I go on the step machine for 15, do inner and outer thigh, and then I do 100 sit-ups to this one song – 'Rude Boy' by Rihanna. It's perfect. I had a phase where I'd been to see a personal trainer – but at the time I wasn't into it. It's only now I've started figuring out what it was I should've been doing and at last I'm nearly where I want to be. I try and go to the gym about three times a week. I know when I've done the workout properly because I feel like I'm about to die at the end of it.

**JEN** I've got ten songs that I turn up if I ever start to feel like I'm flagging, including 'Knock You Down' by Keri Hilson and 'Best I Ever Had' by Drake. For me it's mainly R&B, which is great because they sing about big butts and I'm like: yeah, baby!

**JORGIE** I do dance classes as often as I can fit them in around work. Oh and swimming – I go with my mum and we do races because we're really competitive.

---

**JEN** I know what I need to do to keep in shape – which is stick my iPod on and do loads of cardio. I should also be doing weights and resistance work so I can tone myself up but I can't be bothered at the moment. [Laughs] In an ideal world I need to go about four times a week.

**CLAIRE** I find the gym really frustrating – I get bored easily, so classes work for me. I have quite a fast metabolism – probably because I was a gymnast for ten years.

**GEMMA** She was British Champion!

**CLAIRE** [Embarrassed] I guess my background does help me a bit but I still notice when I haven't exercised. I'm used to having muscle on my body so I always hate it when it goes a bit jelly-like.

**GEMMA** I'm used to going to the gym about three or four times a week – I really enjoy it. And I've got a fantastic personal trainer who works me really hard. She's changed my shape a lot since I first started on *Hollyoaks* and it's made me feel really good about myself. Every so often you need to change the exercise you do otherwise your body gets used to it. But it's about getting a balance because at first I was too strict on myself and didn't have any treats or anything to look forward to. Now if I want something I'll have it.

# Wobbly bits

## " There are some amazing body shapes on set – they are all spot on "

*Jorgie Porter*

---

**Does your weight fluctuate much?**

---

**JORGIE** Yeah, if I'm on my period I'll go much bigger and I'll feel it too. [Grabs her tummy] Jiggle jiggle! I get mega moody just before I get my period. But then when I'm on it I'm just so happy for some reason.

**HOLLIE** She's always happy!

**GEMMA** My weight has fluctuated in the past – I was really thin when I was very young, then when I got to about seven or eight years old I got quite chubby. I got a bit slimmer around the age of 16, but when I joined *Hollyoaks* I put on about a stone in weight – partly because of all the tempting food in the canteen here. I've worked out how to maintain my weight now, though. I go to the gym regularly and I manage to stay pretty much in proportion and now I'm more toned – well, nothing wobbles too much. That said, I would certainly never go to an exercising extreme. I simply don't get the whole size zero thing at all.

> " I hate my legs and my bum. But if I look at myself in the shower, in the mist, it makes me look better! "

**JEN** My weight is always going up and down. But I'm not the sort of person who stresses over their size, I've learnt to accept that that's just me. I think the most attractive thing about a person is when they're confident and happy, no matter what size they are. Any girl can look good with the right make-up and clothes, but it's confidence that makes someone beautiful.

## Do you have any cellulite?

**JORGIE** I've got loads of stretch marks on my bum from when it suddenly expanded when I was a teenager – I'm conscious of them but it doesn't stop me showing people they're there! I'm always getting them out – it's like a party trick. I have cellulite on the back of my legs too. It doesn't bother me, though – that's life, isn't it?

**JEN** Yes, I'm aware of that. I had it from when I was about 16. The only time I didn't have it was when I got stupidly thin and that's not realistic.

**CLAIRE** I don't go looking for it – it's not one of my rituals! But I think every girl has it and you have to live with it. Some have more than others but we all live in our own body so it's subjective, isn't it?

**GEMMA** I've got cellulite but hasn't everyone? It's absolutely fine. It doesn't bother me at all. Unless I'm having a bad day.

**JEN** The other day I went to this really posh shop in Liverpool and there was someone in the changing room so I just started getting undressed in the main shop – I'm not shy. I was there changing in front of people and I knew full well that the women in there were staring at my legs – not as perfect as the airbrushed pictures they'd seen! And I just thought: go ahead and look, it doesn't bother me. [Pauses] Still, if I could get rid of my big bits here [grabs the sides of her thighs] . . . I would. I often look at myself naked and put my hands over those bits to imagine what I'd look like without them.

**" I was 'Rear of the Year' at school! It's weird because I never used to have much of one then one day I had this shelf emerge at the back of me! "**

## How do you feel when you look at yourself naked?

**GEMMA** I feel pretty content. If I'm feeling a bit funny I'll just make sure I cover up for a couple of days until I feel nice again. [Laughs]

**HOLLIE** I hate my legs and my bum. But if I look at myself in the shower, in the mist, it makes me look better!

**CLAIRE** Oh you know – I look at myself and think: I wish that bit wasn't like that. I have my moments. For me it's a lot about the time of the month. I look at my boobs when they're a bit bigger and I like them when they're like that and I have twinges of wishing they were like that all the time. But then my arse is a bit more wobbly then too so there's a trade-off!

## What are your biggest body insecurities?

**CLAIRE** The crease between your bum and legs that never seems to get toned.

**HOLLIE** My worst body parts are my bum and legs because I can never shift weight off them.

**GEMMA** My problem is when I start scrutinizing different parts of my body rather than the overall package. Because when you look at the whole you realize it's actually OK. It's all in proportion.

**JEN** The bits on the sides of my thighs! But then I know they are part of me – and my bum needs them to hold it up!

**JORGIE** My worst part is my belly; I can never get it flat. And when I was at school I looked at all the other girls and they had six-packs but I just couldn't get mine to go down. It has no tone. I have some defined muscles in other places like on my back and I think: yeah! Cobra back! But I can never understand why it doesn't work for my tummy. I've never ever been able to target that area.

## Do you discuss your body worries with your boyfriend?

**JORGIE** Yeah, he likes to touch my potbelly because he says it makes him feel better when he has a bit of a paunch!

**CLAIRE** I've said stuff like, 'What do you think about this part?' and they always say, 'I like you as you are.' So I don't make an issue of it.

**JEN** I might say, 'I'm feeling a right podge today,' but that will be about it. I won't go into too much detail about it. Boys don't get it and if you point it out you are drawing attention to it.

**GEMMA** I always talk to Ian about my body worries. Nothing's sacred in our house! If I'm due on I get a bit of a bloated tummy so I'll stand there in front of the mirror saying, 'Oh god, I need to stop having chippies!' He'll just look at me and say, 'Never mind,' then ignore me and carry on watching TV. A few minutes later he'll say, 'Do you want a chippy?' and I'll be like, 'Oh go on then.'

## What bits do you like best about yourself?

**JORGIE** I like my hands. I've got quite long and elegant fingers.

**HOLLIE** I like my tummy the best because it's quite flat. But the rest of it's a bit shit really.

## What do boys think is your best attribute?

**JORGIE** My bum. I was 'Rear of the Year' at school! It's weird because I never used to have much of one then one day I had this shelf emerge at the back of me!

**CLAIRE** If I'm honest, boys generally like my bum; it's quite in proportion to my shape so as a package it looks OK. It'll do!

**JEN** Most men I've been out with have liked my rear. No one's ever said anything negative – I wouldn't be with anyone who did!

**" If I'm honest,
boys generally like
my bum; it's quite
in proportion to
my shape so as a
package it looks
OK. It'll do! "**

**HOLLIE** Even though I like my boobs I never find any men who are boob fellas. I've never attracted a guy who thinks big boobs are that sexy – they always like big bums.

**GEMMA** For me it's definitely the boobs – all the boys I've been with have loved them. My fiancé loves my boobs and my bum. When I got to about 17 I decided I wanted a breast enlargement – it's not that I hated myself when I had smaller boobs, it's just that they'd never really grown as much as I wanted them to. It wasn't a rash decision; I knew I really wanted them done. I left it until I was 21 and then I had the operation and I loved the result straight away. No regrets at all.

**JORGIE** Mine are quite small but I like that – I don't mind my boobies. I did used to want to have them bigger, but I couldn't afford a boob job at the time. I've stuffed my bra with chicken fillets though. I don't think my boyfriend notices that much until we get home – and then I take them out and he says, 'Oh . . .' [Laughs]

**JEN** I'd actually like my boobs to be a bit smaller – mine are a 32C. I don't like big boobs on me.

**CLAIRE** I'm fine with mine, as much as I go on about them being bigger – I'm pretty content with how they are.

**HOLLIE** My relationship with my boobs is quite good actually – I don't always wear a bra. I have my nipple pierced and once someone looked at me onscreen and said, 'Hollie-Jay – you can see your nipples!' One of the wardrobe ladies told me I need to start wearing a bra. [Shrugs] I quite like my boobs.

## What do you think of the other girls' bodies on *Hollyoaks*?

**JORGIE** There are some amazing body shapes on set and everyone seems to know what their body needs and wants – they go to the gym a lot and tone up. Gemma has an amazing body, Jen has a fab womanly figure and Claire is really athletic. They're all spot on.

**HOLLIE** Claire has an amazing toned figure, Jenny has the most womanly figure, she's gorgeous and pulls off having that JLo booty so well. But I have to say Jorgie has the absolute ideal figure – she's got little legs and a tiny bum that's like a shelf.

**JORGIE** Why thank you!

**HOLLIE** She's gorgeous and tiny and petite.

**JEN** I'm obsessed with checking out other women's bodies. Big, small, tall – they're all brilliant. I went to see *Chicago* at the theatre once and I was open-mouthed at the dancers. They all had lovely little neat figures. But it's not realistic for everyone to look like that.

**CLAIRE** I'd say I'm athletic, Jen's curvaceous and sexy and Gemma's a bit of both.

**GEMMA** I've got curves but I've still got muscle tone.

**JEN** I just think we're a big bunch of different girls and it's good – some have got big boobs, some have big bums – I think it's brilliant. I never think: I'd love to have your figure, though. It would be stupid because I'm me and I'm never going to be like that. Saying that, Claire has a very good figure naturally. We all have our insecurities though.

**HOLLIE** I probably have more than the others . . .

## What do you mean?

**HOLLIE** I'm really self-critical. If I look at myself in the mirror for too long my nose looks out of proportion to my face and one eye looks bigger than the other. Sometimes I'll get to the stage where I think I look so awful in the mirror that I just won't go out. I get really angry and pissed off. The worst is when I'm pale and haven't done my fake tan – I feel the fattest when I've got no tan. People do sometimes find it hard to understand my insecurities because they'll say, 'What are you talking about? You're thin.' But that's like trying to tell someone who thinks they're ugly that they're pretty. It's like Lily Allen once said she looked in the mirror and thought she was Michelle McManus – it didn't matter what anyone else was saying to her, that's how she felt. All my friends have got really good legs and I've never had what I consider good legs. I've always found boyfriends who like my bum or my legs but I have never understood why.

## How hard is it when you have body insecurities?

**HOLLIE** Once we were shooting an episode for *Hollyoaks Later* and I was at a real low about myself. I was with Claire and Jorgie – Claire who has an amazing figure, so toned and boyish, to me it's perfect, and Jorgie has the cutest little figure with the best curves in the world. We were all talking about exercise and our bodies in between takes – and I just stood there listening to them and felt like absolute shit. I felt really fat and really horrible. I said, 'I hate myself,' and burst out crying. That was the result of a massive build-up for me. It wasn't a pleasant experience. It was the result of going home from work every day and feeling crap about myself, thinking I was so ugly compared to the rest of the girls – and it just had to come out somehow. I would look in the mirror every day and think: I don't know why you look like that. No one else looks like that . . .

## What did the others do?

**HOLLIE** Claire just looked at me and said, 'Are you OK?' I think they were all in shock. Jorgie was saying, 'Hollie-Jay, Hollie-Jay! What's wrong?'

## How do you turn it round?

**HOLLIE** I'm OK at the minute because I'm going to the gym a lot – about three times a week. I feel so much better when I've been. Going to the gym is so good for your mental health.

# Golden girls

## " I went on sun beds every week when I was at school "

*Gemma Merna*

### What do you think about tanning?

**CLAIRE** I'd never go on a sun bed. I'm too fair. I went on one once but felt really claustrophobic. I'm pale and freckly so I know there's no point. It's dangerous and people should be aware of that.

**JORGIE** I used to go on the sun bed a lot when I was about 14. Everyone used to do it; I went about twice a week and got so addicted that teachers would say to me, 'Jorge – you look like a tomato!' I'd sneak out of the house having asked my mum to lend me some money to go to the shop and then I'd come back and she'd say, 'Have you been running? You're really red.' I did it up until I was about 16. I wish I hadn't now; I am convinced I'm getting wrinkles!

**GEMMA** I was really bad with them too. I'm very naturally pale but I got really bullied at school about being so white-skinned. People would look at me as if I had to have a tan. I just wanted to fit in. I was put under pressure because people would go under sun beds nearly every day after school and get all brown. I'd copy them but would just burn and go red. It's so dangerous.

## Fake or real?

**GEMMA** I always use fake tan now, without fail. The thing that's important to realize about real suntans is that they fade, but wrinkles and sun damage won't. I did a feature for a magazine in which I put my face under one of those special cameras that show sun damage. I was shocked, especially by the hidden freckles underneath your skin. That shows the damage there is. I can honestly say I'll never go on a sun bed again. You only get one skin and you need to look after it. That's why I always have to go and get spray tans.

**HOLLIE** My fake tan and beauty night is Thursday without fail. But it always starts on a Monday where I'll scrub the remainders of the weekend's tan off. By Thursday I'm ready – so I'll shave my legs and slather on the tan ready for the weekend. Of course that also means I have the fake tan odour when I go to work on a Friday!

**JEN** I'm half Irish so I have naturally very pale skin, which means faking it has always been essential.

**JORGIE** I only use fake tan now, too. My mum really stresses about me going in the sun because I've got a mole on my back that she keeps checking all the time. My boyfriend has to put up with a lot – he tries to talk me out of it and convince me I look good white – because when I've put it on I always say, 'Don't touch me!' [Laughs]

**GEMMA** Ian always gets a line of fake tan across his belly from where I lie across him. And it goes all over my hands and wrists; you can probably see it now.

**JEN** I am such a perfectionist. I can't even get my nails done in a salon because there will be something that will do my head in about it and I'll have to get them off. I have never had a wax either – I convince myself that they'll miss a hair and it would stress me out – so I do it all myself. Likewise with fake tan – I've done it so much that I know exactly what I'm doing!

## OK then, what's the perfect way to apply?

**JEN** I think people are scared of exfoliating and that's actually the most important thing you should do. You need to scrub in order to keep your tan even. I have a little routine: I exfoliate and moisturize every day. Then I apply the tan on my body, boobs and everywhere else, keep on rubbing it in until there's no moisture left. I get my flatmate Mel to do my back then scrub my hands about four times so I know they're clean. Then I put a blob on the back of each hand and use the other hand to rub it in so it doesn't touch the fingers! That's the trick! They still smell like biscuits or curry for 12 hours, though.

**CLAIRE** The worst thing is when you get fake tan in your armpits. It's disgusting!

# Hair trials and tousles

## " I bleached my hair so much it fell out "

*Hollie-Jay Bowes*

.................................................................................................
**What hair disasters have you had?**
.................................................................................................

**JEN** When I was at school I used to have my hair so long and straight I looked like Morticia Addams! It was right down to my bum. Then I decided to have two red streaks either side of my face and this fringe that came out like a sausage roll. It took me about 45 minutes every morning to get the fringe right—

**CLAIRE** Or wrong!

**JEN** [Laughs] I used to curl it and tong it because I wanted it to stick out in a certain way and sit just above my eyebrows. I sprayed it so hard that it didn't move. It was so chavvy! I didn't realize how bad it was until I looked back at the pictures. The ironic thing was that I started a bit of a trend. Then I dyed it a copper colour and it was revolting.

**JORGIE** I was bald until I was about nine years old because my hair was so thin. But then when it grew I had all sorts of styles – I dyed it red with black underneath – that's a bit chavvy, isn't it?

**HOLLIE** You could say that.

**JORGIE** I started dyeing it from about 14. Once it was blonde on top and ginger underneath! You know when Victoria Beckham used to have it short and spiky at the back? It was all choppy with a long bit at the fringe. I idolized her so much I had it cut like that to look like her. After that I bleached it and it all fell out, so I had to get extensions. It's just tinted and toned now so the condition isn't bad.

**CLAIRE** I think I'm having a hair disaster now! [Laughs] Playing Jacqui McQueen means my hairstyle has had to stay the same since I started. Every morning when I sit in the make-up chair I have to have my hair scraped back with these two bits sticking out at the sides. Once upon a time I used to be able to have fringes and soft layers. But now when I'm at the hairdressers they actually have to separate the bits out at the side and work round that.

**HOLLIE** I'm always having hair disasters! When I was 16 and started *Hollyoaks* I dyed my hair myself and it was yellow, brassy and bitty. I used to actually pick out which bits to dye – ugh! Once I started earning a bit of money I went to the hairdresser's. But the more I went, the whiter it got until it was platinum. I didn't realize it had changed so much from when I'd started the show because it was gradual. But one day the *Hollyoaks* make-up lady said to me, 'Your hair is a completely different colour than it used to be, the producer wants it to go back to being yellow again.' I said, 'I can't go back to having it like that – it was horrible!'

## What happened?

**HOLLIE** I remember looking in the mirror one day and realizing my hair was falling out! It had been dyed so many times that it had started breaking off in my hands. I felt like shit – it was just snapping. It got so bad there was even a tuft at the top of my head. So I went to the producer and showed him and it was decided that I could get a wig. I don't think he wanted to be responsible for more hair-dyeing disasters! So that's what I've had ever since. It's good in a way because it means I can do whatever I want with my natural hair underneath – I don't need to keep it to the character Michaela.

## What about when you were younger?

**HOLLIE** My barnet was just a big ginger frizz with cane rows!

**CLAIRE** I once asked my mum if I could have my haircut like Princess Diana. It was hideous. Then I had a bob, then came the phase where you'd spray your fringe into a big bump on the top of your head – a bit like Jen's by the sound of it.

**JEN** The sausage-roll fringe!

**CLAIRE** Yep. It was quite a popular look in West Yorkshire.

**GEMMA** I had a fringe cut once and afterwards started trimming it myself. I did quite well for a couple of months, but then I began hacking at it so much I'd lost sight of where it should be and by the end it was way above my eyebrows! So I had to pin it back and pull the rest of my hair over to cover up the tuft.

**CLAIRE** I also asked my mum if I could have it permed and she said, 'No, here's some benders,' and gave me those funny worm-like rollers that I had to sleep in. I looked baaaad! I went to school with a little mini Afro.

**GEMMA** I'm naturally dark so I had my hair dyed blonde from when I was 15, but I never did it myself. My mum is very glamorous – I never saw her without make-up on – so she took me to a proper salon and had it done for me.

# Too much make-up?

## " Guys find me much sexier without make-up on "

*Jennifer Metcalfe*

---

**How do you feel when you've got no make-up on?**

---

**JORGIE** I used to feel minging but now I just feel fresh. I've decided I'm going to try to use less in future. I have to wear so much at work I hardly let my face have time to breathe. But I hate not wearing mascara – I have naturally fair eyelashes so I look bald without it!

**JEN** I love not wearing it! In this job you wear so much all the time that it's nice to have none on for a change. Unless I'm getting properly dolled up, I'll put a hat on, wear no make-up and look like a little boy.

**CLAIRE** I feel really comfortable with none on – especially if I've drunk loads of water and am feeling fresh and soft-skinned. The only time I don't like it is if I'm hung-over and feel all dehydrated and my skin is dry.

**GEMMA** I definitely think feeling confident with no make-up is something that's happened as I've got older.

" I definitely think feeling confident with no make-up is something that's happened as I've got older "

**CLAIRE** My mum's the complete opposite. She rarely puts make-up on. I, however, have bags of make-up, but for me it's more the arty side to it – I like experimenting.

## Would you ever wear no make-up at all?

**HOLLIE** I feel like a bit of a nonentity with no make-up on. As a rule I like to go all-out with the slap and make my eyes really dark for a night out. During the day just a bit of mascara is OK.

**JORGIE** I always wear make-up too. The teachers at my college used to instil it into us that we always had to look our best and if we didn't wear red lipstick at all times we wouldn't be allowed to go into the class! I think it's a good thing, though – as a lady it's important to look groomed.

## Do you remember when you first wore make-up?

**JEN** I remember my friend Laura Oliver used to bring this little brown glitter pot into school. The brush was coming apart at the ends and she used to put it all over her eyelids and I used to think: that's good, that is. So we started sharing this little pot on the way to school. I'd put it on my eyes, on my cheeks and even on my lips as well so it all matched. Laura bought a new one in the end, so she gave me the glitter pot and I thought: this is my life! I would carry it around religiously. That was my first make-up experience, then after that I went through a phase of slapping loads of foundation on and did it really badly. I used to be fascinated watching my mum do her make-up. She had this concealer stick that she told me I could have – but I didn't know what to do with it so I dug it out of the stick and rubbed it all over my face! And I wore black pencil round my lips for lip-liner.

**CLAIRE** [Laughs] You sound like you were like Jacqui is now!

**JEN** I was!

**GEMMA** I first discovered make-up when I was about 14 – my mum gave me this set from Rimmel and it was all brown colours. I spent hours putting it on upstairs then emerged and my mum told me I looked like I'd been punched in the eyes.

### Are you comfortable around boys when you have no make-up on?

**GEMMA** It depends who they are but all the lads at work have seen most of us girls without any slap on – we have to get in far too early to bother with that sort of nonsense! And Ian, my fiancé, has always seen me without any. When I first met him he'd come over and I was always in my tracksuit without make-up on. At home I'm nothing like I am on set – I've got three dogs, I'm always in scruffy clothes! I love to get dressed up for nights out and I've got some amazing clothes but it's more me to be low-key and relaxed.

**JORGIE** I sometimes think my boyfriend prefers me without it. He picked me up from work once and was horrified at my pink cheeks!

**JEN** I think boys find it much sexier. Guys I've been out with have always said I look nicer when it's not like I'm trying too hard.

**CLAIRE** I agree. But it does depend on the boy and the stage of your relationship – because if you're completely into each other then I don't think it matters what you look like, and during those times you feel at your most confident anyway.

### What do you think about airbrushing?

**JEN** I've been on shoots where I was airbrushed so much there was hardly anything real left – then you all end up like clones of each other.

**CLAIRE** I think airbrushing is fine, we all know it happens. People make too much of a big deal of things these days. What's wrong with it? With or without, I'm personally not bothered.

" I feel really comfortable with no make-up on – especially if I've drunk loads of water and I'm feeling fresh "

" I feel like a bit of a nonentity with no make-up on "

**JORGIE** It's OK to cover your blemishes and stuff. And I think for me, it's good to aspire to be someone who looks better.

### But isn't that a bad thing? Some girls might aspire to something that isn't attainable?

**JORGIE** But I'd still rather have all my bits sorted out in a picture. And people even do it on Facebook these days! When you see models you think, 'Wow, she's amazing,' and I like looking at them.

**JEN** But it's good to let people know that a lot of shoots we do are airbrushed and we don't look like that underneath. It's impossible to look that flawless.

**GEMMA** There are probably still some members of the public who think there's this impossible image of perfection out there, which makes them criticize themselves. The *Hollyoaks* girls are attractive, of course, but when you have a make-up artist and a hairstylist on hand every day you're going to look better than you normally would!

### Do you ask for parts to be airbrushed?

**JORGIE** I've been airbrushed in shoots – I've literally begged them to airbrush me, my tattoo for a start – but that's mainly because it's a butterfly on my hip and me and my mum got it together so it's a private thing. My tummy too! Always. I love it when they've done that. I don't need to work at a six-pack. [Laughs]

**GEMMA** I like having a glow on my skin – and airbrushing can give you a look that you couldn't get naturally. But most of the time, if I'm doing a shoot I just ask for a certain photographer who gets me in positions that are flattering, and which mean I don't need to have lumps and bumps airbrushed afterwards. It's about how you stand a lot of the time. Also, that's why I go to the gym because I want to be able to look at a photo of me and know that it is the real me and I've worked at it myself without being digitally enhanced.

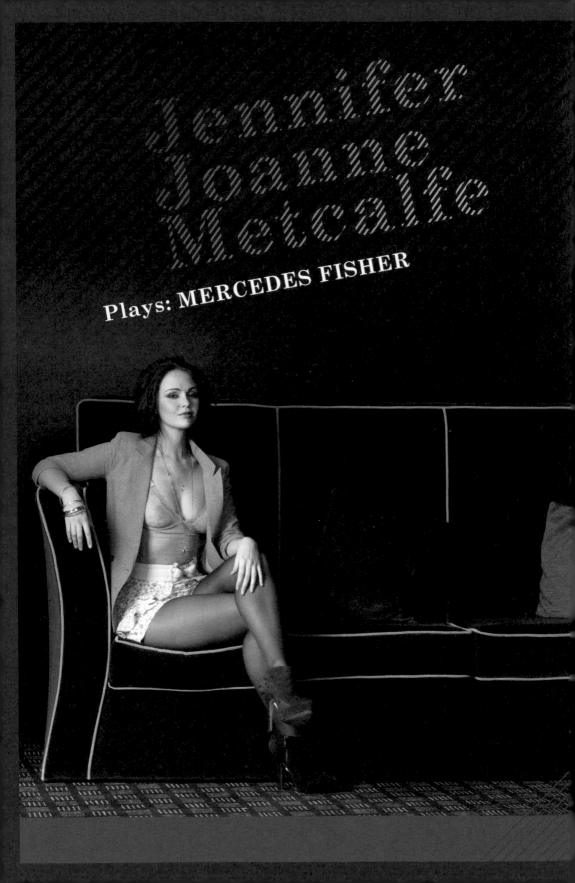

**Birthday:**
04.09.83. I'm a Virgo – I don't read any of that horoscopes nonsense though. Claire Cooper reads them to me and I'm just not interested. [Laughs]

**Most likely to send a text saying:**
'I'm on the loo' – because I'm always so busy that it's the only free time I have! So I'll text my mates, 'Guess where I am!'

**Fave body part:**
My feet. They're dead nice feet.

**Dislike most about myself:**
If I'm tired I'm really stroppy.

**Last lie told:**
I said I was late for a shoot because I was waiting for my dress to dry but I'd actually been watching *Sex And The City* and having a cup of tea.

**Most embarrassing moment:**
I don't really get embarrassed. Although I was on the train once and I was on the phone speaking to my mum and eating grapes. They were these big giant ones you get from Marks

**Bet you didn't know that . . .**
I can burp about half a mile away from someone and they'll probably hear it. And I'm not even joking!

and Spencer's and one got stuck in my throat. I tried to take a big gulp of water but it wouldn't go down – the grape was so big that the water just spilled back out of my mouth! There was a group of pensioners sat in the first-class carriage with me and they were all having their civilized morning tea and I had to go over into the middle of them, gulping for breath and squeaking, 'Help me!' They looked at me and said, 'What's wrong, dear?' But I couldn't speak. I was trying to motion for them to pat my back. But then all of a sudden I just swallowed the grape and said, 'I'm so sorry' and shuffled off again.

**Biggest fashion faux pas:**
I used to always wear spots – I had a full-on yellow outfit. It was spotty socks, a spotty T-shirt, a skirt. Everything had to match. I had a pink and a green version too. Top-to-toe spots!

**My co-stars would describe me as:**
They'd say, 'She doesn't give a shit!' [Laughs]

**Proudest moment:**
I was really proud of myself when I got the job on *Hollyoaks* because before that I was working in a normal 9–5 job and I'd had to motivate myself to leave, get a CV together, try for an agent and focus on what I really wanted to do. I'm not very good at pushing myself so when I look back I'm chuffed I achieved something as big as this.

**Favourite flavour cheese:**
Cheddar or Wensleydale.

**Biggest regret:**
I don't ever regret anything. Everything I've done has been for a reason.

**Most expensive thing I've ever bought (apart from car and house):**
My Rolex watch – it cost me £5,000 and it's gold and stainless steel with diamonds.

**Top three happy tunes:**
That song that goes 'Single girl swag' – it's by Kristina Debarge and it's called 'Goodbye'. And 'Single Ladies' by Beyoncé and 'If You're Single' by Ne-Yo. Songs like that make you feel all empowered.

**My friends call me . . .**
I don't really have a set one; people call me Jen, Jennifer, 'Mush', Grotbags or Gremlin. There's quite a few.

**Last time I cried:**
I'm not generally a crier but I had a real episode the other night. I'd been working really hard and I just think things had got on top of me a bit. I'd gone to Manchester to look in some shops with Claire and when she dropped me back it was midnight and I got to my house but my key didn't work. So I called Claire and said, 'You're going to have to come back for me,' which she did, bless her. We ended up calling all these 24-hour locksmiths and finally one arrived at about 1.30 a.m. We were both knackered. I knew I could've slept at her house but I just really wanted my bed. By

Jen and Lucie chatting in between shots

the time I got inside it was about 2 a.m. and he asked me for £100! I said, 'Seriously?' and managed to get him down to £50 but I still thought it was ridiculously expensive. Once he'd gone, I sat on my couch and I just burst into tears! I was in all my going-out clothes and I sobbed to myself for about three minutes. I don't usually cry, so when I do I like to make the most of it. I was saying to myself, 'Come on, Jen, get some more out!' [Laughs]

**What makes me laugh:**
People falling over and people trumping – I'll howl every time, absolutely guaranteed.

**If I want to treat myself . . .**
I once treated myself and got a new car – but that's on a larger scale! Usually I'll go shopping online – somewhere like net-a-porter and I might get a nice pair of shoes or a bag. Facials are always nice.

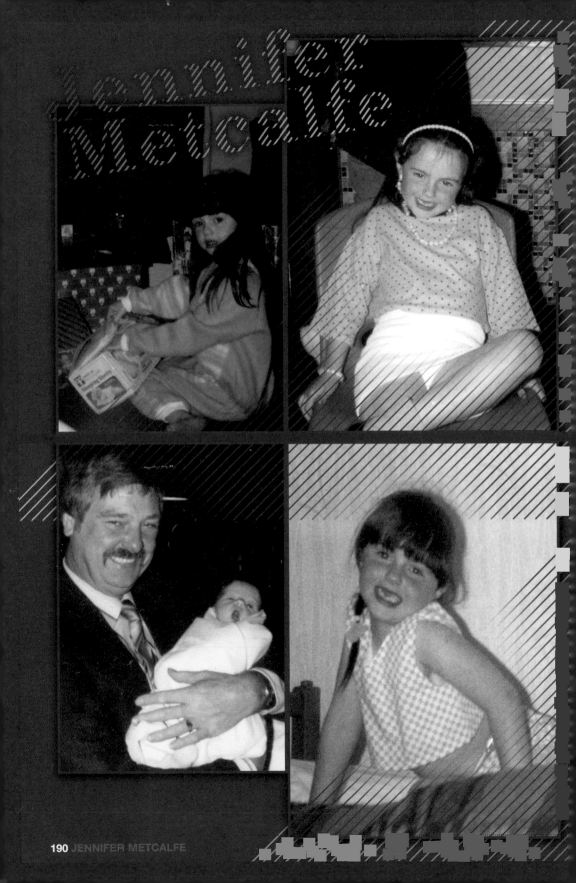

Jennifer Metcalfe

boys, boys, boys

chapter 6

Snogging your neighbour, dating your teacher, getting it on with your best friend's boyfriend, sexting your sister's husband and flirting with your brother (OK, maybe not that one) – these are the sorts of shenanigans that happen every day in the lives of the *Hollyoaks* characters. But as quick as they might be to strip off to their undies onscreen, here we discover just how differently the female stars of *Hollyoaks* feel about boy behaviour when it comes to real life. They chat openly about their failures and successes in relationships, having sex for the first time, good and bad flirting techniques, cringy dating experiences, the pain of being dumped and worrying whether they'll ever find 'the one'.

# Kissy kissy

## " I kissed a boy and gave him a nose bleed! "

*Claire Cooper*

---

**Do you remember your first ever kiss?**

**JEN** Mine was with a boy at school when I was six.

**HOLLIE** [Laughs] What? You were six?

**JEN** Me and this boy used to go into the toilets and say, 'Let's touch tongues,' and we'd do it really quickly then run off. But I guess my first proper kiss was with a guy called Richard who ended up being my first long-term boyfriend. He just grabbed me in the classroom and I remember my belly went all funny. [Smiles] We were together for five years.

**CLAIRE** I was about 15 and was the last one out of my group to get a snog. Amazingly it was with one of the fittest boys in our school. It was at a house party and I'd gone out quite dressed up that night and for once I wasn't looking as geeky as I had been all through school. Either that or he saw through what so many guys hadn't – that I was beautiful underneath! I remember we walked down this garden path and he just leant in.

**JORGIE** I was about 11 when I had my first kiss and everyone else in the world seemed to have kissed and my friends had been pressuring me to do it – but I always said I wasn't ready. But this one day, we went down to this bowling green – it was in the summer and we hid by a bush – and I gathered my friends round and said really dramatically, 'Right, guys, I am ready to kiss someone.' So they took it like a mission, they said, 'We know the best kisser.' It was a guy called Tom Randall.

### What did he have to say about it?

**JORGIE** He just came over obediently and said, 'OK, are you ready for this?' It was all very serious. So we started kissing and everyone counted down from 60. I had my eyes open the whole time.

### What was your worst kissing experience?

**CLAIRE** One guy had a nosebleed on me! I'm really unfortunate when it comes to things like that. Thank god I wasn't doing sexual things at that age – it could've been a disaster.

**JORGIE** The next kiss I had after my first one was horrible! It was at the disco and was around the time where other people would snog five people. I kissed one boy and then he went off and snogged someone else! It was more that I was hurt than anything else.

### What was your first boyfriend like?

**JORGIE** My first boyfriend was the cock of the whole school! He was really hard and a scally and would do wheelies down the road – and it was odd because we didn't even really speak. I didn't really talk to him at school. I was shy. Whenever he came over to me I went red. I thought: I can't kiss you!

**HOLLIE** Mine was a guy called Joe – I was 14 and ginger with corn rows, remember. But I thought I was beautiful because I'd just discovered contact lenses. He was this skater kid and sat near me in Science. I did my hair in these little mini ginger plaits – did them all to one side with the rest of my hair in this big ginger bubble, was really chuffed with it, and then I went over to talk to him for the first time. I said, 'Hi, Joe,' all breathlessly, and he took one look at me and said, 'What is that on your head?' I was so embarrassed! I got home that night and took them all out. Then I bought myself a pair of skate shoes so I looked more like him and literally transformed myself overnight. I took off the Ben Sherman shirts and started wearing more feminine clothes and wooed him into dating me. Even after that I don't think we spoke for about three weeks! Then my best mate was going out with his best mate and we were all watching TV in his room and then we both started snogging our boyfriends. It was like a competition for who could snog for the longest!

**GEMMA** My mum didn't let me have a boyfriend until I was 17 and when I did get one he was seven years older than me. She nearly had a heart attack. I worked in the Trafford Centre at Allsports and he came in one day. I'd seen him out in Worsley where we lived and then we got talking. He was my first love, I was with him for about a year and he broke my heart – it took me about five years to get over him.

**JEN** I went out with my first boyfriend Richard for five years. We were in the same school and for two years nothing happened – we were just friends, really, and I think we were forced together. One of our teachers said, 'You two will get married, you.'

### Do you wish you had married him?

**JEN** He's married to someone else now! He was great though. That's the longest I've ever dated anyone. We were real mates.

# The ex factor

## " It's like someone ripping your insides up "
*Jennifer Metcalfe*

**Have you ever been dumped?**

**JEN** I don't think I've ever been 'dumped' as such. I've always got out of the situation myself because it's not felt right. It doesn't mean the guy wasn't ready to end it as well – maybe I just got there first!

**HOLLIE** I think you can get heartbroken without being dumped.

**CLAIRE** [Sighs] I've been dumped before. He was my first ever boyfriend. I was absolutely devastated. I can't even begin to explain the pain. I was 21 and had been with him for about two and a half years. I've had that pain since but that first time it was unbearable.

**JEN** It's like someone ripping your insides up.

**GEMMA** When I split with my first boyfriend we'd had a little argument and we were that stubborn we just didn't ring each other. It was awful, I didn't eat for days – my mum was trying to feed me vegetable soup and I couldn't stand it. I was crying, 'I'm so upset.' It was horrendous.

**JORGIE** I got dumped but then went to extremes to get him back – everything was such a drama back then! He was my first love and suddenly he didn't want to be with me and I remember causing so many scenes and arguments in public! I think it was because we were both really passionate people. But we always enjoyed making up.

**HOLLIE** All your arguments are dead dramatic! I had a really volatile relationship with a boyfriend and everything was a big deal. Then one day I turned around and I dumped him. I'd had enough.

**GEMMA** It's the worst thing ever when you break up. You're there thinking: OK, what can I do to really hurt him? You're so stupid at that age.

### Doesn't that count at any age?

**CLAIRE** It does for me. I can be ridiculous over men.

**JEN** We all have been, to be honest!

**HOLLIE** I've never been as heartbroken as when I split up with my first boyfriend, Joe. I dumped him and got back with him, dumped him and got back with him. It was such a drama. I remember my stomach was in knots. I lost loads of weight from it in the end. I couldn't eat.

**JEN** That's the thing about breaking up with someone – you can't hold anything down.

### Who do you talk to about boys?

**GEMMA** Jen and I used to live together so we saw relationships break up in front of our eyes!

**JEN** Once she'd had a row with one of her exes and she was walking round in her bra and knickers shouting and crying and I was in my bra and knickers too trying to give her all this serious advice. I was telling her to try and chill out – we must've looked quite a sight.

**GEMMA** I was sat there when we broke up looking at pictures of him . . .

**JEN** Gemma self-indulges, you see. She'll dwell on stuff and make it worse.

## How do you cope differently?

**JEN** I can pick myself up much more easily and move on. I deal with it in a funny way, actually. I don't cry or get upset – I'll just talk it through to death and go over it and over it and keep on repeating myself until I can't possibly go over it any more. Gemma lets me go on a bit, Claire just tells me to pull myself together. Hollie's good as well. Jorgie gives sound advice.

## How quickly do you get over it?

**JEN** About the next day! I actually look forward to when my heart heals because I get a buzz out of wondering who else there is for me – so I'll make myself go on a date and move on.

**HOLLIE** I remember speaking to Jen about a guy I thought she was cut up over. I saw her about a day later and asked how she was and she was like, 'Oh, babe, I'm over it. Done it. Moved on.' [Laughs]

**JEN** You're a bit like that as well, though . . .

**HOLLIE** [Nods] If somebody has messed me about then I can see the bad in them rather than hanker after them like some girls do. The other night I saw my ex and he was slagging it about and snogging other girls. The week before that I'd properly missed him and wanted to get back with him, but when I saw him and he was being a dickhead I thought: I don't like you.

**CLAIRE** Whereas I'll torture myself completely for months . . .

**JEN** [Smiles] She doesn't make things better for herself.

**CLAIRE** I'm my own worst enemy. I have to fully mourn that person before I move on and until that point I don't let anyone else into my life. The best way I can describe it is that I feel they've taken a piece of me and I need to claim it back. It just seems to take me a lot longer than other people.

## Do you find yourself listening to soppy songs?

**JEN** I listen to 'girl power' tunes to make me feel better. After I split up with my ex once I was in a hotel room and the Estelle song that goes, 'I can't be your substitute no more' came on the stereo. Claire was with me and she kept saying, 'I've got a good song for you, listen to this.' There was another one that was good too – what was it?

**CLAIRE** It was a slower one from the 1990s by McAlmont and Butler: 'If you lose me you'll lose a good thing'. That's a really empowering song.

**JEN** I don't like listening to those love songs that make you remember what a lovely time you had and what was brilliant about you being together – I like ones that say, 'You can get lost!'

**HOLLIE** I'm all for that! [Laughs]

**GEMMA** I used to be obsessed with this song that I listened to with my first boyfriend. But it's actually nice now when I hear it because I'm over him and it just brings back good memories instead. I still get that feeling when I hear it, though. It's called 'Drops of Jupiter' by Train. We used to drive round in his car listening to it and then after we broke up I had it on again and again and again.

## Do you find it easy to be friends with your exes?

**JEN** Yeah. You spend so much time with them and do so many lovely things together that it's like falling out with a mate. I've never finished on bad terms with anybody.

**CLAIRE** I'm mates with all of them except my first boyfriend. That's something I've learnt in time, though. It didn't happen immediately. Being friends is a much nicer way than not being friends – unless they've done something really bitter and twisted to you. It's nice to keep in touch because you have a piece of history together. You've shared a lot – why throw that away?

**JORGIE** I don't agree – I think it's hard to stay friends. If you loved someone so much and then you have a new boyfriend, sometimes I feel like it's a bit disrespectful to still be in touch with them. I don't want to forget the past but to me it's about moving on.

**CLAIRE** It doesn't need to be immediate – it might be six months down the line, or a year even. And if I can at some point regain a bit of friendship with them then it makes me feel good because it means I'm over them.

**GEMMA** If Ian was still friends with one of his exes I wouldn't like it.

**CLAIRE** My ex lives in my house with his girlfriend and I'm cool with it. [Shrugs]

**HOLLIE** I'm best friends with one of my exes. We've got a dog together – we're like best friends and absolutely giggle like mad when we're together and we even say we're going to get married one day. We've got the most perfect relationship friendship-wise, it just didn't work as a couple. We don't talk about who else we're with, we just hang out and it's lovely.

# Flirty Gertie

## " I'm rubbish at pulling – I've lost my confidence "

*Hollie-Jay Bowes*

### What's your flirting technique?

**HOLLIE** I fancied this DJ in a club and went over to the DJ booth and thought it was really funny and clever to start playing with the switches on his machine. What was I doing?! I just go the opposite way when I fancy someone and they think I hate them!

**JORGIE** I can't do playing cool. I'm dead obvious if I fancy a guy!

**HOLLIE** I can't either – I've just got this thing now where I let men think I'm absolutely mental when I'm out – I think it's easier. I don't dance in a way that makes me look sexy. I look like a mad person with wings. I think I make myself look too stupid to bother with.

**JEN** When I'm out I like having a laugh with my mates. I don't go out on the pull. I don't like it if someone interrupts on the dance floor.

**GEMMA** I used to scan the room before I met Ian. If I've had a few drinks I would happily talk to most guys if they were polite. Some guys can be a bit cheesy and over the top when in reality there's no need. All they need to do is buy you a drink and listen to what you're saying.

## What sort of guys do you fancy?

**HOLLIE** I like boys who have that indie look, skinny jeans and in a band.

**HOLLIE** I've got rubbish at pulling lately – I've lost my confidence.

**JORGIE** If someone likes her in a club she'll run away! I've had to drag her over. It's ridiculous!

**HOLLIE** It's weird – when I lost my hair back in June because I over-dyed it I think it made me lose confidence. And I haven't got over it. I'm suddenly rubbish with men.

**JORGIE** There was one guy she liked—

**HOLLIE** He was amazing!

**JORGIE** And he came over and started chatting you up!

**HOLLIE** He told me I was beautiful – and I said, 'I'm not, but thank you!' and ran away. I didn't know what to do.

**GEMMA** For me it's important for my boyfriend – or fiancé! – to be a good friend. It's about having fun and always having a laugh. He can't be selfish. The most important thing is laughing.

## Do guys know you're in *Hollyoaks* when they meet you?

**HOLLIE** I get men who pretend they don't when they actually do. But if anyone asks me what I do I'll pretend I'm a student who lives in Liverpool or an air hostess. I went out with this lad for two months who believed that's what I did – so every time I went into *Hollyoaks* I told him I was with Richard Branson. He'd say, 'Where are you off to now, babe?' and I'd say, 'I've got a flight to Malaga,' when in reality I meant, 'I've got a scene and I'll see you in a few hours.'

**JEN** I tell guys what I do – it depends how they deal with it. I don't think it matters that they know you're on *Hollyoaks*, I think it matters how they question you afterwards. If they say that's cool, then it's OK. And as long as they talk about it like a normal job, it's fine. But if I knew that someone was buzzing off me being on it then I wouldn't like that.

**HOLLIE** Me too – it's my idea of hell. I remember a lad coming up to me and saying, 'Sooo! *Hollyoaks*!' and I thought: you've ruined it.

**JORGIE** I always get guys saying, 'I don't watch *Hollyoaks* but that Mercedes is well fit!'

## When you fancy someone, what do you?

**JEN** Special eye contact.

**HOLLIE** Run away!

**JEN** I always think it's good when your mates have gone to the toilet and you're left on your own . . .

**GEMMA** I remember before I met Ian if I fancied someone I'd deliberately not speak to them and talk to their mates instead. Then I'd see one of my mates talking to him a bit too much and think, hey, I saw him first!

**JORGIE** I tried to get my boyfriend together with my best mate! I made them swap numbers but my mate kept saying she didn't have anything in common with him and kept passing the phone to me! That's how we got together!

**HOLLIE** You've set your mates up with your exes too. You're an unusual species who just wants everyone to be happy!

## Do you ever chat men up?

**JEN** I usually wait for guys to come to me but I'll let them know if I fancy them beforehand by giving them the eye and a bit of a smile. One came over to me the other day and he was dead fit. I looked at him and said, 'You've got a good face, you have!' He asked for my number and I said, 'My bag's down there if you can be arsed getting my phone out.' Since then we've been on a few dates and he's great.

**HOLLIE** You've got the confidence – I wish I had some of that.

**JEN** Sometimes I don't, though; I have been a quivering wreck before. But at the moment I can't be arsed and I think because I'm happy being single, men like the challenge.

**HOLLIE** There was one guy recently I saw in a club. I went over and said, 'I think you're beautiful,' and was expecting him to knock me back but he opened his mouth and spoke really strangely, which put me right off. He wasn't cocky enough for me – he was really polite.

**CLAIRE** So you do approach guys!

## Can you ever trust men 100 per cent?

**JEN** No.

**CLAIRE** I don't think men can trust women 100 per cent. You don't know what the future holds or how you're going to change, either. But you can build a tremendous amount of trust if you truly want to.

**JEN** I know people who've been married for years and years and suddenly one of them has had an affair. I think there's too much temptation in this day and age. BlackBerry messengers, Facebook, Twitter – you can contact anyone at any time.

**GEMMA** It means it's so easy for your exes to get in touch with you again or vice versa.

**JORGIE** Sometimes the girls are just as much to blame as the men.

**HOLLIE** I think women find it a challenge to know they've slept with the same person you have. I had that the other night when I was out – three girls came up to me and said they were heartbroken because they'd slept with my ex. One of them even had a tattoo of his face on her leg!

**JEN** Of your ex-boyfriend? That's weird.

**HOLLIE** I know! [Laughs] I was in shock.

**GEMMA** I think people who haven't got good self-confidence are the ones who usually cheat because suddenly they're really flattered by the fact that they have all these options and attention. They like that buzz. I think on the whole men are more likely to cheat whereas women are more settled and happy with their lot.

## Have you ever cheated on anyone?

**JORGIE** No. I couldn't lie about it afterwards, I'm too honest.

**JEN** I could never cheat on anyone. I would get out if I was unhappy.

## Do you ever keep secrets from your partner?

**JORGIE** I've tried but he always finds out. He always finds out about clothes I've bought even if I try to hide them. [Giggles]

# It's a date

## " I set Claire up on a blind date "

*Jorgie Porter*

## What do you wear on a first date?

**CLAIRE** Something casual. You need to feel comfortable and not like you've tried too hard. Saying that, it depends where they take you. If it's somewhere posh, then an evening dress or a nice outfit.

**HOLLIE** I worry more about what my face looks like than my outfit.

**GEMMA** If you have one spot it's the worst – and it always happens just before a date.

**JORGIE** Then you have to spend the night trying to hide your face.

**HOLLIE** And whatever you do, don't eat spaghetti on a first date – I've done that before. I've figured out a method now – when you're going on a dinner date, make sure you've eaten beforehand so you don't pig out.

**JORGIE** I ate half of Tom's dinner on our first date – I was like, 'Are you going to eat that?' and leant over and scoffed his leftovers.

**GEMMA** When you go on a date I don't think the guy needs a lot of money. If someone cooks me a meal that's always much more impressive than spending a load of cash. My idea of the best romantic night is watching *The X Factor* together and relaxing. I don't do that whole fancy thing with candles and stuff. Getting fish and chips in and putting food on a plate – that's romance for me! Why go out to a bar when you've got someone to cuddle up to at home?

## Is there such a thing as love at first sight?

**HOLLIE** I've just decided that if you look you'll never find. You always meet people when you don't expect to.

**CLAIRE** I agree.

**HOLLIE** I've been in situations where I've either been trying to get over somebody else or gone out looking an absolute mess and then it's as if a nice guy has appeared from nowhere. When you go out dolled up to the max, it never happens.

**GEMMA** When I met Ian I'd just moved into my flat and I felt happy being on my own – I didn't really want anyone in my life. I was just content being me. And when he came along I thought: I like him, but I don't know whether I want anything – but I knew I didn't want not to see him again either. If that makes sense! I really wasn't sure. But then he came in handy plugging in my washing machine and doing the DIY! [Laughs]

**JEN** I'd be saying to her, 'What's going on with Ian?' And she'd say, 'Oh he's just coming over to put some shelves up.' [Laughs]

**GEMMA** He'd come round and I just didn't care what I looked like, I was so scruffy – and for once I was me being totally me. I didn't care less. I'd be like, 'Yeah, yeah, that mirror's over there.'

**JEN** At least if you didn't get anything else out of it you got a load of things hanging up!

**GEMMA** I thought he was a bit too quiet to start with but then one day he came over to do something in my bedroom and he'd brought a friend round with him to help. I overheard all this laughing and joking and I went into the room and they were just falling about. I thought: you're actually quite funny. From then on we went on a date, and there you go. [Shrugs]

**CLAIRE** I like to think I played a part in you two getting together. I was Cupid. We were out with Jen and her boyfriend at the time, Jermaine, and Ian was stuck to the pillar for the whole night just sipping his drink . . .

**JEN** I was saying, 'He is so not right for Gemma, he's boring!'

**CLAIRE** Gemma was dancing and just all over the place, ignoring him.

**GEMMA** I wasn't even drinking! I just don't think he knew how to take me to start with.

**CLAIRE** But I could see he really liked her, so I went over to him and said, 'Oh, you know what Gemma's like, she's hard work.' He was just being a bit pissy-pants about it to be honest – he clearly fancied her.

**HOLLIE** He was just nervous.

**CLAIRE** He was! Then the night they first kind of got together I've got a picture of them sat on my sofa.

**JEN** And she looks so uninterested!

**GEMMA** [Laughs] That's because he just bored me! He kept going on about being diabetic and wouldn't shut up. But after that we went out on a proper date to a restaurant and I thought we had a lovely time and got on really well.

**JEN** He doesn't say that now, though, does he?

**GEMMA** No! He said my body language was really bad on that date and he thought I wasn't interested. Then we went out another time and I got drunk and fell asleep on his shoulder – that's when he says he knew, because I must've 'trusted him'. I was just drunk! I remember that night I got into my flat and went into the loo and was sat on the toilet naked trying to take the pins out of my hair. I was shouting, 'Ian! Ian!' and I was wobbling all over the place. I said, 'Can you get me a drink?' and he came in and said that was the first time he'd seen a girl wee in front of him!

**CLAIRE** They're very comfortable as a couple now! I remember soon after they got together – I came up to her flat for a Sunday roast with her mum, dad and Ian. Everyone was talking – and Gemma was sitting on the floor at the time and then all of a sudden this horrendous noise came out of her and there was this wall of silence. I tried to fill in the gap by saying, 'Oh, I do that all the time!'

**JEN** And she never farts! Claire is the most prudish ever!

**GEMMA** It was so embarrassing. It was like when Carrie farted in front of Mr Big – I was hoping the carpet would swallow me up.

**HOLLIE** That's my idea of hell! Keep an element of mystery! I'm not one for pooing or weeing in front of your boyfriends.

**JEN** With me what you see is what you get.

**CLAIRE** I had a boyfriend who was really good looking but didn't really talk.

**JEN** He never said a word to any of us!

**CLAIRE** He was really controlling and would never let me burp or fart in front of him – not that I would choose to anyway. But we were on holiday in India and I could tell it was nearing the end of the relationship. He'd had enough of me and I'd had enough of him – and one day I was in the bath and I thought: we're finished soon anyway, so I said, 'Babe, come here.' He came into the bathroom and I said, 'Watch this!' and I farted in the bath so all these small bubbles came out. He was a goner after that!

**GEMMA** Me and Ian chat to each other when we're in the bathroom – I wish we'd had toilets that face each other so we could talk!

## Have you ever been on a blind date?

**CLAIRE** Jorgie and Tom set me up on a blind date, didn't you?

**JORGIE** He's a real character and funny.

**CLAIRE** They didn't tell me he was off his rocker!

**JORGIE** I thought you'd like him!

**CLAIRE** He's mad. But I went out on another few dates after that so he must've been intriguing.

**HOLLIE** I've never been on a blind date, ever.

**GEMMA** I went on a blind date with a radio DJ once because I thought his voice sounded gorgeous. But it didn't quite match up. Don't judge a man by his voice! [Laughs]

**HOLLIE** I'd like to know what it's like to ask someone on a date – to have that confidence.

**JORGIE** You have to have thick skin – so many guys I asked out in the past didn't want to know me. But you just have to move on to the next one.

# Dressing to impress

## " A man needs to be careful what he wears on his feet "

*Hollie-Jay Bowes*

---

**Does it matter how a boy dresses on a date?**

---

**HOLLIE** Yes! I always look at their feet. There's nothing worse than bad shoes on a boy.

**GEMMA** But when you're like me and you have three dogs that stand all over your feet the whole time and ruin your shoes, I don't think you can judge on shoes!

**HOLLIE** I went on a date with this model who was stunning. When we first met I looked at him and thought: wow! He had a cracking body, loads of amazing tattoos all over but he had really awful shoes. I have a thing about men wearing shoes – they shouldn't. I think Converse look better every time, even with a suit.

**GEMMA** When I met Ian there were things about what he wore that I didn't like but whereas it would've put me off other guys before, I let it slide because I knew there was more to him. In the end you just get over it. You go past that cringeworthy stage. Sometimes you can be put off people too easily and might ditch them because you don't like their shoes or hair without properly finding out if they're right for you. It goes both ways anyway – they might judge you just as badly for something you're wearing or something you do.

**HOLLIE** It's weird how little things can put you off guys. After I'd noticed the shoes I kept seeing other things like his veiny arms.

**GEMMA** Once there was a guy I really liked – and he called me and said he was going to pick me up in this big white transit van. And I was convinced he was going to pick me up in a white van and tried to get my mum to cancel it for me! That's how bad I used to be.

**JEN** I'm usually alright with most guys for about three months. I'll have the best three months ever – the first one they'll be proper buzzing off you, the second I'll be wanting to marry them and then the third I've gone off them!

## Do you fall in love quickly?

**JEN** I don't fall in love so much—

**GEMMA** It's lust with you!

**JEN** I can make conversation or get on with most guys on a first date. But when I look back it's always after two or three months that it's suddenly over in my head. All it takes is a day – something they do puts me off, I can't handle it any more and then everything comes on top of me and I need to end it. I just get rid of them that day!

**HOLLIE** And then she gets another one!

**JEN** All my boyfriends look so different – tall, short, mixed race, white, blond, dark. With me I think looks are about 20 per cent of the package. It's the same with girls as well. If a girl is stunning-looking but a bit of a tit with no personality, then she might as well be ugly for all the use her looks are!

**CLAIRE** I go for something deeper. Men need to be kind of quirky for me – I can't even properly explain what it is.

**HOLLIE** They have to make me laugh.

**JORGIE** Me too. That's the most important. They have to find me funny as well – there's nothing better than a guy laughing at your jokes. It makes you feel nice.

**HOLLIE** I agree. They've got to laugh at me and let me take the piss out of them – that shows they have a sense of humour. Oh, and they've got to have long hair. [Laughs]

# Text etiquette

**" Hollie gets a text from a boy saying, 'Hello' and then asks me, 'What do you think it means?' "**

*Jorgie Porter*

---

**When you get a text from a guy, do you analyse it?**

`HOLLIE` Absolutely. I read them to five different people to get five different opinions so I know what to send back.

`JORGIE` You've forwarded texts to me before saying, 'What do you think it means?'

`HOLLIE` And usually I get the reply, 'He's just saying hello!' But I'm like, 'Hang on, he might be saying hello but he's put two kisses, why has he put an extra kiss?' Honestly I am terrible!

`JEN` It depends who it is.

`HOLLIE` When it's someone you've just swapped numbers with you need to know whether they like you or not and that's when you read into the texts.

`GEMMA` I hate it when there are people you've got to figure out and analyse. Why is it that you want those sorts of men more than the ones who let you know they like you straight away? Why are you so desperate for them when they might only call you once a week and leave you hanging on??

**JEN** I've been watching *Sex And The City* for the first time recently and it's telling me how to deal with men.

## How long do you wait to text someone back?

**HOLLIE** Two hours. I write the message and save it and then send the reply in two hours.

**JEN** I will phone the guy rather than text back, I think it shows confidence. Because if you didn't care that's what you'd do.

**HOLLIE** I'm shit with men, me! I used to be really good. I think I'm unattractive to all species.

**JEN** Stop it, silly!

**HOLLIE** I don't think it helps that I wear a wig at work for a living – I think men find that very strange!

**CLAIRE** I remember being with a guy and I was sat with him at the end of the night, really pissed and – believe it or not – having an intellectual conversation about the world. But I was taking out my hair extensions and throwing them around the room! He just laughed and didn't mind the chaos.

**JEN** One of my exes put two of my extensions on each nipple and one down below and started dancing around! [Laughs]

# Let's talk about sex

**" As soon as I'd done it I thought – I have to tell my mum! "**

*Jorgie Porter*

---

**Do you remember first thinking about sex?**

---

**GEMMA** My mum was a bit of a prude so I didn't really speak to her about it until I got older. I had to find out from my mates.

**CLAIRE** I remember being at a party when I was 15 and two people from our school being in the bathroom and having sex – I couldn't believe it. I couldn't even comprehend doing it. And looking back I still can't. It just seems way too young.

**HOLLIE** I come from a big Catholic family and we're all really open. My mum and I talk about everything – even now when we watch sex and stuff on the telly we talk about it. We cringe at each other – she's amazing.

**JEN** My mum gave me this book called *Growing Up* when I was about 12. That taught me about the birds and the bees.

**HOLLIE** You were sexy at a young age, you were!

**JEN** I could ask my mum anything too, though; she was like my best mate.

**CLAIRE** I wouldn't go and talk about sex to my mum; I used to talk about it between my mates. Luckily my mates were at the same stage as me in that they weren't doing it but we could if we wanted to. We used to chat all the time about what we thought it would be like.

**HOLLIE** And if it would hurt!

**JORGIE** I would just tell my mum everything! The thing is, there's no point trying to hide stuff from her because she'd find out anyway! I also spoke to my best friends Mary and Marie – I was so scared. Everyone had done it before me – the whole school was doing it! They were all really blatant and open about it as well. One couple were really cocky and kept announcing, 'Yeah, we're doing it tonight,' and I kept thinking: that should be a private thing!

## What do you remember about your first time?

**HOLLIE** For some reason, after I'd done it I thought: oh my god, I've got to tell my mum! She wasn't cool about it at all and I thought she would be. I don't think she wanted to know!

**GEMMA** I didn't tell my mum – no way! I get dead embarrassed talking about stuff like that; I think it's a private thing.

**JORGIE** I was with my boyfriend from high school for two years on and off, and it was after Prom night. And it wasn't like I expected at all. Not what it was built up to be. But I was glad I did it with a guy I really liked.

## How do you know when you're in love?

**JORGIE** When you don't stop talking about them all the time and when you relate everything to them, like if I had a bottle of water I'd say, 'Oh, Tom drinks water . . .' [Laughs]

**HOLLIE** When you can't stop looking at your phone.

**GEMMA** You get butterflies, don't you? [Laughs]

**JEN** Your belly goes all funny and you poo a lot! [Laughs]

## How long should you wait before you have sex?

**JORGIE** I'd say a month at least, that's a good time. If you do it before then I always think you're not going to be together long.

**HOLLIE** When it feels right – but not on the first date. That is very whoreish! [Laughs]

**GEMMA** I agree – you should know when it feels right and never rush into anything you're not comfortable with.

## How important is sex to a relationship?

**ALL** [In unison] Very important!

**JORGIE** And the best time of day to do it is when you're out shopping and you look at each other and say, 'Are you thinking what I'm thinking?' and you have to run home dead quick. [Giggles]

**HOLLIE** I don't know if it sounds shallow but it is very important. If it's not there then the intimacy's not there and that's the special part of a relationship.

# Single girls

**❝ I thought I'd met 'the one' twice before. I don't know if I can go through that again ❞**

*Claire Cooper*

**How are you different when you're single compared to when you're in a relationship?**

**JORGIE** I'm tamer. I'm happier in who I am when I'm in a relationship.

**CLAIRE** I sleep more when I'm in a relationship. Don't know why.

**HOLLIE** When I'm in a relationship I'm always thinking I'm missing something.

**JEN** I think I lose myself sometimes when I'm in a relationship.

**HOLLIE** Oh yeah, I think it goes both ways. When I'm single I want to be with someone and when I'm in a relationship I want to be single!

**Isn't that just because you haven't found the right one?**

**GEMMA** I hated those relationships I was in before when you're constantly worrying about what he thinks, or feeling sick and paranoid. But when you're in the right one then it just fits. Don't get me wrong, the first year and a half with Ian was hard – I think it is in any relationship when you're still getting to know each other. There's a lot you have to compromise on – there are things you disagree with or don't want. But when you get past that it can be amazing. We know each other so well. I tell him everything, we're dead open and I know I can be who I am. If I have a problem at work or with anything he'll be the first person I'll call and talk to about it. He knows how to calm me down and make me stop worrying.

**CLAIRE** The older you get I think the guys you meet are looking for someone more serious – you're at an age when you know guys could be looking at you as wife material and it freaks me out, because I don't know whether I am! [Laughs]

## Do you get obsessed with the idea of meeting 'the one'?

**JEN** I feel dead excited about it. I love going out with a new guy and thinking: this could be the unlucky one! [Laughs]

**GEMMA** I was always excited to meet that person too. And with me I was single for so long before I met Ian that it might have something to do with why I was able to settle down sooner than the others.

**CLAIRE** I thought I'd found 'the one' twice. I really did. And it's made me question a lot over the past year that these two people could have affected me so much and I could've got it so wrong. It makes me think I honestly don't know any more. It's made me think about stuff a hell of a lot. It scares me that I don't know what I want from life any more.

**HOLLIE** There's somebody out there for everybody.

**CLAIRE** Yeah, but with me there were two people I could've felt it working with and those things have all been taken from me so I struggle with what I feel afterwards. I now have to protect myself from feeling like that and being in that situation again. We all want to meet the one but I don't think I want to go through what I've been through twice now in 18 months. I don't think I could physically cope.

**HOLLIE** I think I'm just going to go with the flow now.

**JORGIE** I believe that if you wait and are just patient it will happen. It does happen for a reason – you have to enjoy life now.

**JEN** I think it's possible to have met 'the one' a few times – when I look back on my relationships, if I'd met one or two now I probably would've made more of a go of it. It's about timing.

**GEMMA** I know now that me and Ian have been in the same places at various times before we got together. But I never noticed him. It was just that one night that I got out of a taxi going into a bar, and saw him on his phone and he smiled. It was only because he was outside the bar I noticed him – if I'd been inside I probably wouldn't have clocked him because it was so busy and there were so many men about.

# Jorgie Alexandra Porter

## Plays: THERESA MCQUEEN

**Birthday:**
25.12.1987. I'm a Capricorn, like Hollie-Jay. I don't understand it when the horoscopes say things like, 'Your planets are flying this way.' Of course, I do read them and convince myself they're talking about my actual life.

**Most likely to send a text saying:**
'I can't talk, I'll phone you in a minute.' People are always messaging me at the wrong time like when I'm working but because I text them back they think I can talk and text again!

**Fave body part:**
My fingers because they're freakishly long.

**Dislike most about myself:**
I can't organize time to see people. I say I'll do something and then won't be able to because something will come up and I feel bad and disappointed.

**Last lie told:**
'Grandma, what do you mean? I've had this top for ages!' My gran thinks I'm always buying clothes, which I am, so I have to fib.

**Bet you didn't know that . . .**
Once when I was a kid, I decided I wanted to be a footballer. I bought the boots, the shin pads and everything! I did it for about three months. My mum just said, 'OK, whatever you want to do, Jorgie, I'll back you 100 per cent.'

**Most embarrassing moment:**
Chipmunk was on the *Hollyoaks* set for a show and he came over afterwards, put his hand out to say goodbye, I shook it, then he said, 'Come to one of my gigs!' and put his hand out again. I thought: why does he want to shake it twice?, but put mine out again anyway. The thing is, he had sunglasses on so I couldn't see where he was looking and he was actually putting his hand out for the guy behind me! So suddenly there were three of us having a big massive handshake.

**Biggest fashion faux pas:**
When I first got hair extensions, I cut them into different sizes and glued them smack in the middle of my parting on the top of my head. It went all the way from the front to the back!

**My co-stars would describe me as:**
Happy.

**Proudest moment:**
Getting my job on *Hollyoaks*.

**Favourite flavour cheese:**
I love all cheeses; the only ones I don't like are the smelly ones like Stilton.

**Biggest regret:**
Not learning to drive.

**Most expensive thing I've ever bought (apart from car and house):**
A Gucci bag – it was over £600.

**Top three happy tunes:**
Princess Superstar, 'Perfect'; 'You To Me Are Everything', by The Real Thing, and T.I. 'Swagga Like Us': it's a remix and has a sample of M.I.A.'s 'Paper Planes' in it. Proper ghetto and funky.

**My friends call me . . .**
'J', Jorge, Joey.

**Last time I cried:**
I was carrying my big huge Gucci bag around London and it was dead heavy and dragging on my feet and I tried to hail a taxi and no one would pick me up. I was feeling all sorry for myself and shed a few tears.

**What makes me laugh:**
When I have to carry something like a TV – because I'd know that if I dropped it would be disaster. It's like I'm daring myself and I get the giggles.

**If I want to treat myself . . .**
I buy new shoes or a new handbag.

a world of issues

chapter 7

In its trailblazing guise, *Hollyoaks* goes where no other soap storyline has dared. From male rape and self-harming to anorexia and HIV – there is no subject deemed too tough to tackle. Not just pure unadulterated entertainment – sometimes *Hollyoaks* can even teach you something new and interesting. It opens our eyes and minds to things we would never want to imagine happening in our own worlds, and shows us that bad things can happen to good people. *Hollyoaks* manages to both embrace gritty reality and tell it like it is, while simultaneously portraying its characters through bonkers dream sequences, dramatic surrealism, flashbacks and crazy spoofs. It's a soap that relates to us in a way that no other show does and dares to be different. Here the actresses talk about their experiences on the pioneering programme and reveal the secrets behind the workings of the show – from the high drama of their ridiculous fight sequences to emotionally charged scenes and downright silly accidents on set.

# Backstage

**" I didn't know what it was going to be like so I never had any preconceptions "**

*Hollie-Jay Bowes*

---

**Talk me through a typical working day . . .**

**JORGIE** I have a big make-up call so I'm usually in early. Theresa has lots of slap and massive hair! It takes about ten minutes just to backcomb the top of it. There can be up to eight shoots in one day, so you jump from one to another – one second you might be bawling your eyes out and the next you're meant to be dead giddy and laughing. You have to keep track of your character's journey all the time because you might be shooting scenes two weeks ahead, then going back to a scene in the past.

**JEN** Because Mercedes has such glamorous make-up I have to go in early too. The thing that's sometimes difficult about this job is that there's no routine, nothing's ever the same. Sometimes it's a day shoot, sometimes a night shoot. So really your body clock is all over the place. It's like having jetlag.

**CLAIRE** When I get home at night I'll listen to my voicemail from production where they'll tell me which scenes I have the next day. I'll already have read them and filed them away, but if you go through them too prematurely you'll get ahead of yourself and your storyline.

**HOLLIE** I live in Manchester and I drive into work, which takes about an hour and a half. So I have to get up really early. I'm so used to it now that I don't struggle getting out of bed any more. I get to work, have my make-up done, go for breakfast and have a refresh of my lines I'd looked at the night before. Get on set and it takes about two hours to do a one-minute scene – we're single camera so you have to go through every scene from several angles. You do a read-through, a block-through, then a rehearsal, then the scene. We do between eight and ten scenes a day and it will be a mixture of all emotions. One minute it's happy stuff, the next you can be in tears. It's a strange job, when you think about it. For me it could be quite normal to be stood outside in the early morning wearing a bridesmaid's dress, crying.

**JORGIE** The other day I'd had a long day filming and when I woke up the next morning I was still so tired it felt like I was drunk! I have cried from exhaustion before.

**GEMMA** When I joined, I remember Bryan Kirkwood [producer] – who I love dearly – brought me into the office on my first day and said, 'When you start it will be like running into a brick wall. Make sure you eat plenty, make sure you sleep loads,' and he couldn't be more right. I was travelling back and forth to Manchester then as well because I lived there for the first six months. So I was getting up very early to get in on time. My make-up call was at 6.30 a.m.

**HOLLIE** I didn't know what it was going to be like so I never had any preconceptions. When I say to people: I can't come out tonight because I've got to be up early tomorrow, they will say to me, 'You what?' But it's normal to me. I've never known anything else. To me having a lie-in is being able to get out of bed at 9 a.m. But luckily I'm one of these people who can live off little sleep.

**CLAIRE** I am always well prepared and I make sure everything's logged so I know where to find it. Especially if I have a big scene. I don't know if that's just me, or if it's the training that's been drummed into me. I need to know where I'm going, where I've just been and what my objective is as a character. I've got a different accent in the show to my own in real life and I'm playing someone who has bigger energy than me so I'd be a fool not to do my homework. I can't play myself like maybe other people do. What I don't like is when there are changes made on the day. It can happen at any time and really throws me. I get in a little tizz inside because it ruins everything I've rehearsed. But you have to deal with it. I don't like surprises. I have a grumble and then have to adapt to it, there's no time to mess about.

**JORGIE** If someone's off sick the whole day will change – it affects everyone on that shoot. It means new scripts will sometimes get given to people at the last minute because different people have to be brought into the scene. It's very complicated! I've had a scene where I've been given a whole page to learn about ten minutes before I'm due to go on because things have changed around so much. It's hard not to get stressed and nervous about it, but you have to stay calm otherwise you're in trouble!

**CLAIRE** We did a scene where there was an explosion in a church when Niall had kidnapped the McQueens and Jacqui had loads to say – pages and pages. And on the day they said, 'Can you take that line, that line and that line out  – and put that word there?' and I looked at them and said, 'No.' I didn't have time to readjust it. So they replied, 'Fine, we'll do it in the editing suite.' And that really offended me because I'd spent a few nights perfecting those lines.

### And you shoot things in random order . . .

**JEN** You lose track, especially when you get in really late at night or early in the morning. Sometimes you don't get a chance to do all your research. The other day I'd been working so much I got on set and said to the director, 'Where am I and what am I doing?' But it's just the nature of the job.

**CLAIRE** At the moment I have about 15 scripts to go through and we always shoot out of sync. I'm used to it now, but it's still a little odd whenever you film what happened next before you film what went before!

## Do you ever forget your lines?

**JEN** Yeah, I did it yesterday! You panic and think, I can't do this, but you end up doing it just because you have to.

**CLAIRE** I did a national tour and was playing the female lead for a year and I didn't miss one show, but I became so tired and run down I got shingles. I'm generally quite a happy person and a busy bee but when I get tired or emotional I can get stern and businesslike about stuff and it can get misinterpreted. Then I have a moment and get all teary because of how I've said something.

**GEMMA** It's not like a 9-to-5 job. I think when you join a soap like *Hollyoaks* you don't realize how hard it is, and no one around you does either. All my friends and family think it's just very glamorous and it's not – it's amazing and gives me so much back, but you're constantly on call so you could be brought in at any time. Which means you never truly have a day off, in a sense. Depending on your storyline it can be constant. I haven't had a full weekend off for the past seven weeks so it's knackered me – and when it's heavy stuff emotionally, it's even harder.

**JEN** With me, I'm my own worst enemy. I work hard and so I think I'm going to play hard too, when really I should think: you're working so hard you need to give yourself a rest. I can't do it any more. I've burnt the candle at both ends too often!

## But it's a glamorous life, isn't it?

**JORGIE** It is when you get to go to parties, or the fact that you're looked after and pampered a lot of the time. But when it comes to things like filming outside in the freezing cold and pretending it's summer because you're filming two months ahead, and you're naked and people don't understand how freezing you are, that's when you think: this is not glam.

# Keeping
# it real . . .

**❝ I feel really close to her as a character but I don't always agree with her ❞**

*Claire Cooper*

---

***Hollyoaks* has tackled a lot of issues in the past . . .**

**JORGIE** The one I remember most is when Gary Lucy's character got raped in the show. That really stuck out. I feel proud I'm on a show that tackles so many hard-hitting storylines, and kids can look up to you and know there are people going through the stuff they do.

**HOLLIE** The anorexia storyline sticks in my mind. I think it's such an important issue. People can be harsh on each other; it's as if they think they can just tell someone with anorexia to eat more and that'll sort it out. There are clearly emotional issues underlying it all – you can't be that way for no reason. And I think it's great that a programme like *Hollyoaks* was able to highlight that.

---

**When you're acting, do you draw from experience or instinct?**

**JORGIE** Sometimes you'll have to act situations you have never touched on in your own life, so in those instances you need to research it and imagine how your character would feel. It's good to watch as many films and read as many books as you can. But then you have to be careful you're not getting too influenced by how other people interpret emotions, you need to go with your own intuition.

**GEMMA** I work a lot from instinct. There was the six-month episode when Carmel's husband Calvin dies – he's shot in front of her – and I've never ever had to experience that, thank God. When I came into rehearsal I had to hold back a lot of the emotion – I'd made myself think about that happening to someone really close to me but I knew I could only let the emotion out properly for one take. I really felt that feeling. And I said to the director, 'I can only do this in one take.' So we rehearsed about six times and I wouldn't let myself get into it for real, then we got it in one take. I was so happy with my performance in the end. Everyone in the room was crying when they were watching it. I burst into tears when I watched it back too. I don't really put myself in the experience – I put Carmel there and I work out how she must feel.

**HOLLIE** For me, I don't have that many life experiences to channel into my acting, to be honest! I've had a few deaths in my family – my nana died when I was twelve and my granddad died last year, but they're the only big things. And I wouldn't say that they've helped me with scenes, though, because I would never channel that energy. I have to put Michaela there. There was a scene when Zak cheated on Michaela and that has never happened to me so I was struggling with it. But I had to just go there and be her and deal with how she would feel.

**CLAIRE** I don't think it's safe to rely on emotional memory. It's not a safe way to act because you could get yourself into a bit of a state before the scene. It's about tapping into elements of those emotions and using them.

**JORGIE** During the storyline when I was with Tony I imagined how I felt when I was first in love. I drew on all the feelings I had with my first boyfriend and what I went through, how much I cried and how it hurt when we argued.

**There was a storyline of Newt cheating on Theresa with her best friend. Has anything like that ever happened to you?**

**JORGIE** No, but I think I would deal with it in the same way she did – you've done wrong, forget it. That's it. I wouldn't be able to stand for it either.

**GEMMA** A storyline can really affect you. When we did the church explosion scenes and Niall had the McQueens all tied up, we were just filming in a dark room all day, and as soon as I got home I had to go straight to bed because I was so exhausted. I was in tears and Ian said, 'What's wrong with you?' I couldn't answer him. I didn't know why I felt so low.

**What was that particular storyline like to film?**

**GEMMA** It was incredible. It was a long day's filming and it was both emotionally and physically draining. And we work to such tight schedules that it's impossible to spend as long perfecting a scene as you'd like. It also means we end up losing shots that have been planned because we have to move on in the schedule – and sometimes scenes you've worked really hard on will be cut. But actually Carmel's so happy most of the time that the most serious issues she has to face are usually to do with boys. And in a way they're probably the easiest ones to relate to!

**CLAIRE** The losing the baby storyline was powerful for me – I knew that so many men and women had been through it that I had to be sensitive. It was interesting for me to play because it was the first time people saw the real raw side of my character. The sort of person Jacqui is means you only get about a 3 per cent window into what she's really like. It was challenging because I wanted to depict it in a truthful way as so many people out there have been in that awful situation. The feedback I got was really good – I had lots of letters from women who had lost their babies thanking me for my portrayal. And when Jacqui married the Albanian, Alex, because she had to – she was being bribed – that was quite interesting.

**You've had some tough storylines as Jacqui . . .**

**CLAIRE** Another one that sticks in my mind was when she asked her sister Tina to be surrogate. Tina was played by Leah who's one of my best friends, so that made it more emotional. Tina wanted the baby back and there was a lot of heartache doing those scenes – I remember Leah bawling her eyes out and it was really painful to do. But nobody sided with Jacqui on it. They thought she was selfish. I don't think she was. I think the viewers needed to see more of Jacqui's point of view. But we have to follow the script.

**What about the scene in the church when Jacqui's mum Myra chose her to die out of all the kids?**

**CLAIRE** I enjoyed that script. I asked my own mum if she'd be able to choose between me and my brother! But it was tough to do the scenes. Jacqui couldn't forgive Myra. Jacqui's been through such a lot and didn't have the childhood the others had because she was bringing them up. But she'd die for her family. I feel really close to her as a character but I don't always agree with her. And when I don't agree with certain scenes morally, I struggle, because I can't understand her motives.

**Hollie, was your onscreen band anything like your real band?**

**HOLLIE** No, nothing like it! [Laughs] My onscreen band was a lot of fun but it wasn't anything like my music taste. There was only one song. I did worry I would look a bit gimmicky afterwards because I'm really serious about my music in real life and I didn't want it to come across like I was a joke. But luckily it didn't last.

**What about that *Hollyoaks* music show where Daniel Merriweather made you cry?**

**HOLLIE** His song 'Red' was around when my granddad died. It's such a beautiful song and moves me whenever I hear it and I don't really know why. He was performing on stage and I knew he was only allowed to play two songs, and then the second one kicked in and it wasn't 'Red'. I thought: he can't come here and not sing 'Red', that's just not allowed to happen. So I got the crowd to start chanting 'Red! Red!' at him and he looked really embarrassed and mumbled, 'I can't, I'm sorry – there's no time.' Then we all started singing the song to him and it got louder and louder. And all of a sudden he came in a cappella and it went, 'I can't do this by myself' and I burst into tears! Everyone was laughing at me and saying, 'You fancy Daniel Merriweather,' but I didn't. It was just that song. I get the same feeling when I listen to 'Moondance' by Van Morrison. I love that song. I always say that's going to be my wedding song. It reminds me of my dad – I used to listen to Van Morrison's album with him when we travelled down to Birmingham every Saturday to see my sisters. I used to know all the lyrics.

### Do you find it easy to make yourself cry on set?

**HOLLIE** I tend to find that if I yawn first it helps. It makes it easier because your eyes are already watering. But you have to channel something really horrible to get that crying. Some people can't do it at all – they really struggle. But to be honest for me it depends what mood I'm in. There was one day when I just thought: please don't make me cry today, but I had to for the scene and came away feeling so drained.

**JORGIE** When I first started I found it really hard to cry because I was so happy about being in the show! And they said, 'You have to cry' – I remember being told during the Tony storyline that I had to cry more, and I used tear stick a lot. But now I've got much better for some reason. The first time you cry in a take is always the best one – so it can be frustrating when you have to do it another eight times! But I've learnt how to channel my emotions more now and take myself to a different place a lot quicker.

**CLAIRE** I find it hard to do it time after time – which you often need to because, like Jorgie says, the take they end up using is always about the eighth one! When you're in the moment on the first or second read it's far easier to conjure up the emotion but it's towards the end that the tear sticks come into it. There was one scene between me, Gemma and Nicole around the time my character had lost the baby. One of my lines was, 'Mum, I've lost my baby,' and it was so poignant that we all just burst out crying on the read-through! Even the PA did. I don't know what had happened but it really affected us – the others said it was the way I said the line. And the director was going: 'Quick, get the camera on them now!'

## What's a tear stick?

**CLAIRE** It's a bit like Vicks or Olbas oil and makes your eyes naturally water. But when I'm in a scene with Nick Pickard I genuinely cry – and I make him do the same. He's my tear stick! The other day we knew it was one of our last scenes together for a while and his lip was properly quivering when I was speaking to him.

## What's it like doing fight scenes?

**CLAIRE** As Jacqui I seem to have loads! I'm always fighting someone or they're slapping me. We're allowed to slap each other for real but the fight scenes are choreographed. Me and Steph, who plays Cindy, had a great fight scene in one of the late-night episodes, which we worked out with the stunt person on set. You have to formulate a proper routine because the cameras need to know which shots are coming next. It was great, though – we were really buzzing off it.

## How do you get into the zone when you're filming a more serious scene?

**CLAIRE** I have to stay away from everyone, prepare myself, clear my thoughts and feel the emotion. When we get our script that's usually the first time we know that something's going to happen, which doesn't always give you a whole lot of time to rehearse! I like it when a director gives you the licence to think of different ways to act a scene out and allows you to take risks.

**JEN** I loved doing the storyline about Mercedes having an affair with Calvin. When I first saw the script, though, neither me nor Ricky Whittle thought it would work. We thought it was unrealistic for our characters to fall for one another. But once we started filming we knew we had something and I've been really proud of the work we did with it. The HIV storyline with Malachy was tough for me because it was not something I could relate to. I did some research for the part initially, but then I thought: maybe I don't want to do too much because Mercedes needed to stay ignorant about it. It was hard, and so draining, but the resulting scenes are things I can be proud of for the rest of my life.

### Has it ever happened that you've had to do a happy storyline while feeling sad?

**JEN** One time it did. I was so upset in my personal life. And I had to do a scene with Nicole [Myra McQueen] and Mercedes was sitting on a sofa eating a banana and she was laughing and joking. I had to be the happiest ever. I didn't think I was going to be able to do it because I felt so miserable. All I wanted to do was cry in a room – but I had to be fun-loving Mercedes. I don't know where I dug it out from but I got there. I watch it back, though, and it was a brilliant scene.

# Best bits

## " Ricky Whittle pulled a moony while I was doing a take "

*Jorgie Porter*

---

### What's your character like to play?

**JEN** Mercedes is common, sassy, thinks she's better than anyone else and believes she's gorgeous. I used to think she was a tart with a heart but to be honest I don't even think she has a heart any more – I think she's a bit of a bitch! She's tacky but I love playing her.

**CLAIRE** Jacqui represents a lot of chavs, and I think she represents them very well! [Laughs] She has tremendous loyalty, she's snarly, comedic and she's three-dimensional now. At one point she was just shouty but she's got more substance, which I'm proud of.

**HOLLIE** I'm a lot more responsible than Michaela. She's like me but when I was 12 years old. She's just never going to grow up.

**JORGIE** Theresa is a girl who's fascinated by older men. She's the sort of Lolita type, and doesn't think about what she's doing or that getting with them is a problem. She's really flirty and she's really big-headed about how attractive she is. She'd be a nice friend but would probably steal your boyfriend!

---

**JEN** I think Mercedes is emotionally unstable.

**CLAIRE** I don't think Jacqui is, surprisingly. I think no matter what's happened in her life she keeps trooping on. She's a wounded soul but she's strong. She went to jail because Mercedes didn't cover her back.

### Have you watched your first episode back?

**CLAIRE** [Cringing] I did and hated it! I look the same but my acting is shocking – so much has changed since then. I think at first I was trying too hard to be this huge character and a real madam, but two months into it I knew I had to make her three-dimensional and for me that's when the character was born and she became more interesting. I learnt to play her down a bit and make her softer in moments. Sometimes I like to play with the directions a bit – so if the script says, 'Jacqui is angry', I'll twist it on its head and play her more calmly so it has more of an effect. And then when I'm not meant to be angry, I'll explode in one of the lines.

**JEN** My mum came round and so did a few friends and I remember thinking: oh god, I look rough! [Laughs] But I enjoyed it. We had a really good director who helped me through it so for a first episode I didn't think it was so bad. I'd like to see it again for a laugh. Nowadays, I don't make a point of watching past episodes but if I'm at home and *Hollyoaks* is on then I'll stick the TV on.

### Do you criticize yourself?

**JEN** Yeah! I'll always have a check of how I look to start off with and if I look alright I'll enjoy my acting. If not, I'm pointing at the TV saying, 'Eurgh! Look at the state of me! What am I doing?'

### What storylines stick in your head as being the most fun?

**GEMMA** My best storyline was when we were filming Carmel's first wedding and I had to be spray-tanned! Claire was there as Jacqui

> **"We used tea as the tanning liquid and I had it all over me. It stunk!"**

with her marigolds on and one of those spray bottles you put weed-killer in. We used tea as the tanning liquid and I had it all over me. It stunk! I was there with my underwear on dancing about. I love playing the funny stuff because that's what Carmel's all about.

**HOLLIE** There was a storyline in which Michaela wanted to adopt five puppies but she has to choose between the dogs and her boyfriend, who's allergic to them. So she chooses Zak and I had to cry my eyes out when the dogs go off in the van. It was comedy gold.

**JORGIE** I love doing the naughty things with the other 'kids' in *Hollyoaks*; they're the most fun. It's good being able to put a school uniform on again too – and it just makes you instantly feel peskier!

**GEMMA** Oooh! I also loved the episode when Carmel was arrested for being a prostitute. Then she got put in jail and I had a cameo with

Bonnie Tyler who appeared to me as part of a dream. When I found out she was going to be in the show I was over the moon – I wanted to kiss the producers!

**JEN** We did a scene where the McQueens were shoplifting and pretending to be pregnant as a decoy, which meant we had massive bumps.

**CLAIRE** It was hilarious and we had to film it in the Met quarter in Liverpool, which meant there was still public about, they hadn't closed it off or anything – it was so embarrassing!

**JEN** And we egg each other on by pulling silly faces.

**CLAIRE** I think the McQueens should go on a trip to Las Vegas! It would be amazing – can you imagine how chavvy it could be? Someone could get married by Elvis. We could all be on our slot machines in our tracksuits! Come on, producers!

## Who are your favourite people to work with on *Hollyoaks*?

**CLAIRE** I love working with all the McQueens because we have a united front, we know each other so well and I trust them 100 per cent. And I love working with Nick Pickard. I think our characters are interesting together and we really buzz on screen. I love a person who's passionate about what they're doing, and he is. He's very professional as well and knows his lines – there's nothing worse than people who don't remember or don't care!

**JORGIE** The McQueens! Genuinely. When we're all together it gets to the point where I'll have a line and I'll forget to say it because I'm so busy watching them. I'm so engrossed. I'm thinking: this is really funny stuff. And then they'll be waiting for me and I'll go – 'Oops!' It's like a real-life play!

**GEMMA** Ricky Whittle is amazing because he always makes me laugh. I think it's actually nicer working with a boy because they're never on their period so their moods aren't quite so changeable. He's never down, always upbeat. We just have a laugh and play-fight. Out of the girls I like working with Claire. I think Carmel and Jacqui are such a good double act – Claire's comedy timing is great.

**HOLLIE** I agree. I love working with Kent Riley who plays Zak – we've got a similar sense of humour. But at the same time we can handle each other when we're in a mood. He tells me, 'Shut up, Hol, you're being a knob!' And he can tell me where he thinks I've gone wrong in a scene, which I like – we learn from each other. He can say, 'Will you play your scene like this for me so I have a little bit more to go off?' and I'll think: great.

## Are the boys troublesome on set? What are they like to work with?

**GEMMA** Glen Wallace who plays Malachy is hilarious; Kent Riley who plays Zak is so silly and makes people laugh all the time. He'll read his lines but add so much more in like swear words and stuff – which makes us all crack up. He ends up making up the whole scene and we end up in hysterics. We are like a little family, which is lovely.

**JORGIE** Kieron Richardson is amazing. He's so good to work with and such a great actor. He's fantastic – not like his character Ste one bit. Nick Pickard is funny too – he has no spatial awareness whatsoever. He stands on your feet – he's always bumping into things! And he's funny in that he'll just start singing opera or musicals onset. He's hilarious.

**HOLLIE** Kieron is amazing, as is Kent – he's mental. Me and Kent have this thing where we try and get the word 'ham' in a sentence. Claire's involved too. But because it's a funny word it ends up as a noise at the end of whatever you're saying: 'Hmm.' It can get repetitive on set so we like to have things to amuse ourselves. And I love Quinny [Anthony Quinlan who plays Gilly] to pieces – I remember we got snowed into a hotel once. *Hollyoaks* had to put us up in one because we both lived in Manchester. And we hadn't socialized before but because we had access to the hotel bar we ended up getting rat-arsed. By the end of it, it was about 3 o'clock in the morning and we were in my room laughing our heads off, talking about absolutely everything. We had to be in work the next day!

**JEN** All the boys on the show are brilliant. Kent is so funny – he always makes me crack up. Ashley Taylor Dawson who plays Darren is great too, and I love working with Glen, who plays my husband Malachy, because we can have proper chats. They're all ace.

**JORGIE** Ricky Whittle pulled a moony at me when I was doing a take – and I had to have a serious face!

*Hollyoaks* **is the only soap of its kind to employ 'dream sequences' and flashbacks – what are they like to film?**

**CLAIRE** Some of them really work well and prepare people for the episode but there are some I just look at and think: I don't get it! We did one where we were all in court and there was a brilliant shot with a light over my head. I like the darker, weird stuff because it looks more edgy. I remember there was a film noir one, which I wasn't involved in but looked so cool. And we did a good one where all the McQueens were playing bingo. The camera panned along us and we didn't know what each other was doing but when we watched it back it was so funny because everyone was different and pulling a face that was so true to their character.

**GEMMA** I've done millions of dream sequences – they're dead funny. We did one where all the McQueens were in *Oliver* – Claire was the Artful Dodger and I was a policeman. It's nice because you get to have a little bit of a play about with make-up and clothes.

**HOLLIE** It's like a big bit of fancy dress. It's ace.

**" One minute it's happy stuff, the next you can be in tears. It's a strange job, when you think about it. "**

**"** I want everything now and I'm always in a rush, but I think my 50-year-old self will be much more chilled **"**

*Jen*

past, present & future

## If you could go back in time and speak to your teenage self, what would you say?

**JORGIE** I would tell myself not to try and be everyone's friend. I used to be obsessed with trying to be liked and making everyone happy. But now I know it's not possible, people don't always click with you. I'd tell myself: don't worry about it, not everyone gets on with each other. It's about acceptance. Accept how tall you are, accept what colour hair you've got, accept yourself and just grow with it.

**CLAIRE** [Laughs] Stop worrying about everything so much. I must've spent a good few years worrying and I don't think it's healthy. It apparently causes illness so I'd better stop.

**HOLLIE** I'd say: shut up and get on with it! Don't question anything, keep your mouth shut and don't burn bridges.

**JEN** I always think I did what I did at the time for a reason, so I think I'd be proud of who I was then. If I said anything it would be: don't have so many tears over men, because ultimately it doesn't matter. When the right one is meant to come along, he will. I've wasted a lot of tears over the years, so I'd tell my teenage self to get a grip and get on with it.

**GEMMA** I'd say: don't listen to other people. Jealously is the most evil thing ever and other kids will say things about you to put you off your goal. I used to sing a lot at school and bullying really affected my confidence and made me not want to get up on stage. Be who you are.

## Now imagine you're 50 years old. What is your life like?

**JORGIE** [Laughs] I'll be living abroad with big massive glam hair and fake nails, lots of little puppy dogs running around and a young toy boy cleaning the swimming pool. I've got loads of Botox! Loads of surgery, in fact. Everything will have been done to keep me all perky.

But I'd still have a few wrinkles so people could tell how old I was. [Giggles] I'll be happy with what I've achieved in life, and I will have travelled all over the world.

**JEN** I'd probably be haggard because I've been on one all my life! I hope I'm married with a kid and have a lovely house in somewhere hot with a yacht. I hope I've been really successful. Would I have surgery? Yeah, probably. [Laughs] I'll have a bit of a glow, slightly shorter hair, maybe in a bob, and I hope I'm dressing quite sophisticatedly. I hope my body takes after my mum's – she's 60 this year and still has the tiniest waist. She's like a better version of my figure.

**HOLLIE** I'm living in a cool bricky apartment in New York. I've also got a pad in Paris and one in Tokyo. I've still got wacky pink hair and have two dogs. I'm a successful musician/fashion designer. [Laughs] I live for my career and wouldn't let anything get in the way of that. I am Botoxed all over – I am not growing old gracefully! I have the perfect husband, he's my age and is a musician. And we've got cool kids who all wear Converse.

**GEMMA** At 26 I've achieved a lifelong dream for many people as it is! I've got an amazing home life and job and great friends. I couldn't wish for anything more. I might have more animals and I'd like loads of children to look after me when I get older. I might be living in America. I'd love to be a casting director – I think it's important to give people chances. A lot of us got in *Hollyoaks* because the producer and casting director took a chance on us. We hadn't done much before and they took a risk. I'd like to give others that chance.

### Any surgery?

**GEMMA** [Laughs] Yeah, probably! I don't know if I could go through with a facelift but I'd like one. I'd have a few nips and tucks, a few injections here and there – let's just see.

**CLAIRE** I hope I'm really happy. I hope I'm lucky enough to have a child and I'm still acting. I'd like to have been in some Agatha Christie dramas and maybe go back to the career I had before *Hollyoaks* – I did some good dramas, like *Waking the Dead*, so if I can carry on in that vein and do some theatre I'll be very satisfied with my lot. I think I might be living abroad, maybe somewhere in France. I don't think I'll have surgery. I think if I was going to have a boob job I'd have done it by now. I hope I'll have aged nicely and be comfortable in my skin.

### What do you think your 50-year-old self would say to your today self?

**JORGIE** I'd probably say: make more effort with your friends and plan to see them more. If I don't still know my friends when I'm 50 I'll be absolutely gutted.

**HOLLIE** I'd probably have the same advice as before – shut up and stop burning bridges! Try not to let things and people bother you so much. And get yourself more focused.

**GEMMA** My mum always says you don't know your own mind until you're 30 and she's probably right. I'm 26 and I've always had an older mind than most of my friends. But I think by 50 I'll be pretty wise and have plenty of advice to give myself!

**JEN** Slow down and take your time! I want everything now and I'm always in a rush, but I think my 50-year-old self will be much more chilled.

**CLAIRE** I'd probably tell myself to chill the hell out. Seriously. Give yourself a break, love!

# and finally

**If someone has just picked up this book and flicked straight to the back page, how would you like them to know you?**

**JORGIE** 'Enthusiastic and passionate. Small and blonde.'

**CLAIRE** 'Quirky, generous and quite pensive at times but confident with it.'

**GEMMA** 'I'm very loyal and honest but don't take the piss with me.'

**HOLLIE** 'I'm just a bit weird. Sorry.'

**JEN** 'I'm a normal girl who knows how to make the best of herself. I've learnt that looks are only 20 per cent of what makes someone attractive. Confidence is what makes someone beautiful.'